HOMEMADE SOUPS

HOMEMADE SOUPS

Elisabeth Luard

Photography by Ian Garlick

MQP

Published by MQ Publications Ltd
12 the Ivories
6–8 Northampton Street
London N1 2HY
Tel: 020 7359 2244
Fax: 020 7359 1616
E-mail: mail@mqpublications.com

North American office
49 West 24th Street
8th Floor
New York, NY 10010
E-mail: information@mqpublicationsus.com

ISBN: 1-84601-144-2
978-1-84601-144-3

1 3 5 7 9 0 8 6 4 2

Printed in China

IMPORTANT: Those who might be at risk from the effects of salmonella
poisoning (the elderly, pregnant women, young children and those suffering
from immune deficiency diseases) should consult their GP with any concerns
about eating raw eggs.

Contents

Introduction

The very idea of it warms the heart—the scent of it, even the sound of it bubbling gently on the back of the stove, releasing in soft puffs the delicate fragrance of herbs, underpinnings of onion and parsley, the sweet perfume of celery and carrot. And then, at last, there's the taste of it—the sheer pleasure of that first spoonful. When there's soup on the table, all's well with the world. Comforting, wholesome, simple to make, and a pleasure to eat, soups appeal to the heart as well as the appetite, satisfying both body and soul.

Soup dishes can be found in every corner of the world—there are Chinese soups, Indian soups, African soups, Italian soups, Spanish soups, English soups, and American soups, to name a few. These range from simple soups designed to make the best of a single seasonal ingredient to more complex soups flavored with a dozen different ingredients. And, soups aren't just for starters. There are warming healthy soups to soothe the ill, hearty soups that can be served as a main meal, festive soups prepared for religious holidays and family celebrations, and inspired soups made from yesterday's leftovers. The best soups, however, are those created with those extra special ingredients, whether it's the soup you made on the day your home-grown tomatoes achieved perfection, the chowder cooked with fish so fresh it jumped off the slab, or the tasty broth you left to simmer overnight.

At its most basic, soup is one of the easiest dishes to prepare. Anyone can make a soup, with or without a recipe. It's a dish for all seasons, enjoyed by everyone, eaten at any time of the day, in company or alone, as a sophisticated dish or a simple light lunch. Soup recipes are also remarkably flexible considering how ancient they are: When the New World potato replaced the chestnut in the soup pot of the Old World, no one complained.

Soup is the ultimate comfort food and this isn't just down to the ingredients, but also in the way it is served. The size and shape of the bowl and the material it's made from, whether it's porcelain, china, metal, or wood, will all affect the flavor of a soup. There's nothing ostentatious about a soup, however luxurious (well, even a lobster bisque speaks of maximum use of crustacean-debris). You can be sure that whatever you decide to throw into the mix will give all its goodness to the broth, both in terms of flavor and nutrients. Creating your own soups is also economical, especially when

prepared in large quantities—you can eat some now and freeze the rest. If you prefer to cook ahead, you can make the broth today and serve it tomorrow.

A good soup can be converted into a meal in itself with minimum fuss: Team a vegetable soup with a plate of salami, ham, or with a thick slab of cheese. The Germans follow a robust meat soup with something substantial in the way of dessert—a strudel or a fruit-stuffed dumpling. The Greeks turn a fish soup into a satisfying meal with a salad of ripe tomatoes and feta. With more substantial soups, one can serve these up as two or even three courses, a practice common in Spain and Portugal, where the broth arrives first, to be followed on the same plate by the vegetables and pulses, with a final course of meat and potatoes, and all cooked together in the same pot.

The lighter soups, those prepared as a starter to a menu, particularly clear broths and consommés, lend themselves to fancy finishings: A swirl of cream, a dollop of garlic mayonnaise, a spoonful of pesto, a handful of croûtons fried in olive oil with garlic or crisped in butter with bacon, a sprinkle of toasted almonds or pine nuts. Unclarified broths can be fortified with noodles or dumplings, as in the soup traditions of China and Japan, or with pulses, rice, or rice-shaped pastas, a tradition common throughout the Middle East. There are also the stand-alone soups which are designed to feed the heart as well as the belly: The robust bean-based soups of the Iberian and Latin American tradition, creamy fish and potato chowders from both sides of the Atlantic, and France's stupendous meat and vegetable broths.

While soup can be eaten at any time, in the context of a formal menu, its place has traditionally been at the beginning of a meal (though certain sweet soups are placed at the conclusion). In China and Japan, soup continues to take its place in the middle or at the end of a formal meal, and also serves as a fortifier. It was from the evening meal of rural France—*le souper*, a simple meal of broth poured over bread—that soup acquired its modern identity, moving to a supplementary role rather than the main event. Although eating heartily at midday and lightly in the evening is the healthiest option, the business-day has changed our eating habits. The timetable altered when people started to work in offices and factories and took to eating a light meal in the middle of the day, shifting the main meal (the traditional midday dinner) to the evening. In the transitional stages, those from affluent families took supper, a light refreshment usually consisting of a clear broth or a milky caudle taken before bedtime. As the work day became more arduous and people no longer went to bed at midnight, lighter and more elegant soups began to appear at the start of the evening meal or (as confirmed by the popularity these days of soup bars in cities) as a midday snack with bread. At the same time, hearty soups, such as Italy's minestrone, the *cocidos* of Spain and Portugal, and Russia's borscht, remained traditional midday fare for the rural labor force.

Great soups, the classic soups whose fame spread as a result of the appearance of regional cookbooks, remain firmly rooted in their place of origin: Peanut soup is what you'd expect to be served in Ghana, a *laksa-lemak* is what you'd hope to find in Malaysia and chicken soup with dumplings is standard fare in Jewish households. Many of these traditional recipes have been adapted to suit modern tastes. Restaurant chefs continue to re-create traditional recipes in forms which suit their clients, taking their lead from the great French chefs of the 18th and 19th centuries, innovators of haute cuisine, whose work marked the moment in which soup recipes became more inventive. These days, veloutés, consommés, and single-vegetable soups—aristocrats of the soup-maker's kitchen—are served as something to amuse the palate, a demonstration of the cook's skill, a way to awaken the appetite and sharpen the taste buds for pleasures to come. Creativity is always welcome: Many of the celebrated soups of modern times are the result of experimentation. Who would have thought that ginger would taste so good with carrot? Or that a cauliflower soup might be transformed by the simple addition of cumin? Both these happy combinations, and many others, are of very recent invention.

The soup recipes in this book are simply those which have earned their popularity because they taste so good. As for the recipes, no need to follow ingredients to the letter: Choose what looks good at the market today and adapt the recipe to suit. When picking your raw materials, favor those which have been produced as close to home as possible. Treat weights and measures as a guideline rather than a straitjacket: Herbs are of varying strength, fish and fowl as well as meat and beans are uncertain in the amount of time they need to cook. No one can claim the definitive recipe for, say, a Louisiana jambalaya or a Scotch broth or even that maid-of-all-work, the French pot-au-feu. And nor, wisely, will we.

Soup-making is personal, there's the beauty to it, so set the pot on the stove,
stir up a storm, and have fun.

Soup Techniques & Tips

Soups for different seasons

There are soups for all seasons: Warming soups for winter, light soups for spring, chilled soups for summer, and wholesome soups for the fall.

In spring, when the first young vegetables come into the shops, stir green leaves—young spinach, shredded hearts of young cabbage or lettuce, lemony sorrel, aniseed-flavored chervil—into a bean or potato-based soup for freshness of flavor. Such soups go well with spring salads—new potatoes dressed with olive oil and chives, baby tomatoes tossed with basil and just a pinch of sugar, a well-minted tabbouleh with plenty of parsley dressed with lemon juice. Take advantage, too, of the shellfish available—oysters, clams, and mussels are plump and full of flavor at this time of year.

In summer, go for creamy soups that take well to chilling: Vichyssoise, watercress, carrot, or pea soup finished with sour cream. Serve the classic cold soups of the Mediterranean—red and white gazpacho, yogurt, and cucumber—well-cooled in the refrigerator and refreshingly diluted or sample one of the fruit soups from Northern Europe—blueberry, cherry, or apricot—served cool. Fish soups are perfect for a summer supper, from the mighty bouillabaisse to a simple Greek avgolemono.

In fall, choose vegetable soups to deliver the sweet maturity of harvest—pumpkin, squash, corn, sweet potato, chestnuts, wild mushrooms, and apple spiced with cinnamon. As soon as the nights grow chilly, turn your thoughts to the dhal-based soups of India, delicately spiced and eaten with freshly baked flatbreads. Appropriate, too, at this time of year are the elegant noodle soups of China and Japan; light but nourishing, they're particularly delicious when finished, as in south east Asia, with shrimps, green chile, and coconut cream.

As winter draws near, go for the robust bean or lentil soups which remain the mainstay of the farmhouse kitchen, or choose one of the rich meat or poultry, or bone-based broths which can, with the addition of root vegetables and pasta or dumplings, be served as a meal in themselves. When entertaining friends during those wintry evenings, start your menu with a well-flavored consommé, or a sophisticated crab or lobster bisque, or one of the single vegetable soups—tomato, beets, onion—which sharpen the palate without dulling the appetite. This is the perfect time, too, for the milk-caudles, syllabubs, and egg-thickened sweet soups.

Soup-making equipment

You need very little in the way of special equipment to make a soup, and you'll probably find that you have everything you need in your kitchen already. A saucepan of 2–3-quart capacity, with a heavy base to discourage burning, is essential. You will also need equipment for the initial preparation, such as a small sharp knife or potato-peeler for vegetables, a chopping knife, and chopping board. A measuring jug and a set of cups will also come in handy, and a skillet will often be required to prepare ingredients for the pot. If you intend to make your own broths, a large capacity stockpot is also essential. As for finishing equipment, you may find that you need a food processor or blender if the soup is to be reduced to a puree, as well as a strainer. The alternative to both these pieces of equipment is a mouli-legumes, an instrument which looks like a fine-holed colander equipped with a flange, a flat piece of metal which fits into the rim of the colander; the flange is turned with a handle, pressing both solids and liquids through the holes and leaving any chewy debris behind.

Serving soup

Hearty soups are best served directly from the pot in which they're cooked, although a tureen (pre-warmed with boiling water) is also an option if the cooking pot is not as elegant as you'd wish. Wide-rimmed soup plates (also pre-warmed) are good if the soup has suckable debris—shells, bones etc. that need to be removed from the dish—and for main course soups served as more than one dish. Bowls (pre-warmed and chosen for compatability with the recipe) are good for purees and other debris-free soups. As a general rule, a one-person serving is around 1 cup, though the volume should be halved if you're serving the soup as the starter. Most recipes in this book serve 4–6 people, depending on appetites and setting.

Storing or freezing soup

The most convenient way to store a basic stock is to reduce it to half volume, pour it into ice-cube trays, allow to cool, freeze until firm, then pop the cubes out of the trays and store them in bags until needed (they'll last for at least 3 months). Simply drop them into boiling water to bring them back to life as a tasty stock. Remember to label the bags—there's nothing more irritating than finding you've defrosted a fish stock when what you need is chicken. Clear soups and broths can be stored in the refrigerator for a week in a covered container—just give the broth a good boil before using. They can also be frozen as above. Thick soups should be well cooled before storing in the refrigerator and should be used within 2–3 days.

Chopping vegetables

You can be guided as to which knife to use by the size and shape of the vegetable you are about to prepare. A large, knobbly celeriac is best tackled with a medium-sized, non-serrated blade, whereas a tomato yields wonderfully to the pressure of a incisive knife with a serrated edge. Bunch your fingers together to hold the vegetable in place, while you slice away with the knife in the other hand. Here's a selection of some of the most popular vegetables and how to chop them.

DICING PEPPERS

Cut off both ends of the pepper. Make a cut from one end to the other and open the pepper out into a long strip. Trim off the white pith, remove the seeds, and cut into strips. Hold the strips together and cut into dice.

DICING CUCUMBER

Peel the skin off with a small, sharp knife or vegetable peeler and cut in half lengthwise. Run a small sharp-ended teaspoon down the center to remove the seeds. Cut into long strips, then into dice.

SLICING TOMATOES

Use a knife with a serrated knife and sharpen it well before attempting to cut the tomato. Depending on the type of tomato and the recipe, remove the watery seeds and any tough flesh from the stalk end.

CHOPPING GARLIC

Put the unpeeled garlic cloves on a board and place the thickest part of a chef's knife on top. Smash down with your fist to break them, remove the papery skin, then chop finely, rocking the knife back and forth.

CHOPPING SCALLIONS

Trim off most of the green part of the scallion and cut a small slice off the root end to remove it. Run the point of a sharp knife down its length several times, then finely chop across the shreds.

CHOPPING SQUASH

Cut off the peel with a small sharp knife or vegetable peeler. Cut in half and scoop out all the seeds and fiber in the center. Cut each half into wedges, then chop each wedge into pieces.

CHOPPING PARSLEY

Employ the two-handed method for chopping parsley finely—indeed for chopping any herb. Hold the knife by the handle and the tip and rock backward and forward. Or snip herbs with scissors held blades downwards.

SLICING EGGPLANTS

Trim the ends, then cut into slices. Eggplants used to need salting to bring out the bitter juices, but this has been cultivated out of newer varieties. If you do want to salt your eggplant, put it in a colander, sprinkle with salt, leave for 10 minutes, then rinse.

Chopping an onion

The secret to chopping an onion lies in the root end. In here is the substance that makes eyes stream, and the trick is to avoid cutting into this section. First, cut the onion in half through the root end and tip, using a large chef's knife. Use the blade to ease off the brown papery skin, then cut the tip end off both halves.

STEP 1

Make sure you leave the root end intact. Take the point of the knife and make incisions, starting just slightly away from the root end, down to the tip end.

STEP 2

Make several cuts across the onion half, again not quite reaching the root end. Two or three cuts should be enough, but it depends on how small you want your onion slices.

STEP 3

Using the uncut root end as a sort of handle, cut across each onion half to make onion dice. When you reach the root end, simply throw it away.

BASIC STOCKS

The stockpot is the soupmaker's secret weapon. In the days when large households ate together at least twice a day, the presence of a large pot bubbling gently on the back of the cooker ensured the cook had the basis for a nourishing, healthy, economical meal. Meat and vegetable trimmings, bones, scrag ends of ham, chicken carcasses, all these were popped in the stockpot to reinforce the broth along with enough water to replace what was removed on the day. These days, smaller households, irregular mealtimes, and changes in the way people actually buy their food—meat off-the-bone, fish in the form of fillets, ready-trimmed vegetables—have made it increasingly difficult to set up a proper old-fashioned all-in stockpot. As a rule of thumb, reduce any stock you mean to keep to half its volume before you freeze it in an ice-tray. Remember that chicken, meat, and vegetable stocks can be used interchangeably—the only one that is truly purpose-built is a fish stock—and since miso is already in ready-prepared form, a miso soup is best made up on the day of use.

Vegetable Stock

Makes about 2 quarts

2 large onions, finely chopped
2–3 leeks, thinly sliced
4–5 ribs celery, diced
1 fennel head, diced
2 large carrots, diced
2 bay leaves
1 thyme sprig
$\frac{1}{2}$ teaspoon black peppercorns
$\frac{1}{2}$ teaspoon sea salt

1 Put all the ingredients in a heavy stockpot. Add 4 quarts of water and bring to a boil. Turn down the heat and simmer for 1 hour, or until the volume is reduced by half.

2 Allow the stock to cool and keep in a covered container in the refrigerator—it will last for 4 days, but is better used as fresh as possible.

Chicken Stock

Makes about 1½ quarts

2 chicken carcasses (raw or from a
   couple of roast chickens) or 3
   pounds chicken wing tips and necks
1 large onion, quartered
3–4 medium carrots, cubed
1–2 leeks, chunked (include the green)
3–4 ribs celery, cubed
5–6 parsley stalks
½ teaspoon peppercorns
   (preferably white)
2–3 allspice berries
1 level teaspoon sea salt

Tip
A chicken stock should be
pale and clean flavored. This
needs long, gentle cooking and
constant skimming to remove
impurities which would
otherwise drop back
into the broth.

1 Break up the chicken carcasses, removing any fat or flaps of skin. If using wing tips and necks, rinse them well. Pack all the ingredients in a large stockpot and add just over 2 quarts of cold water.

2 Bring to a boil, skim off the gray foam that rises, turn down the heat, and cover the pot loosely, leaving a small opening for steam to escape. Simmer very gently for 3-4 hours—for a perfectly clear stock, the surface should tremble, no more. Skim the fat from the surface every 20 minutes.

3 Strain out the solids, return the stock to the pan, and bubble up until slightly reduced.

4 Let cool, lift off the thin layer of fat which has solidified on the surface, and store in a covered container in the refrigerator for no more than 4 days. To keep for longer, reduce the volume to 1¼ quarts (the stronger the stock, the longer the shelf life) and freeze in ice cube trays.

Fish Stock

Makes about 1 quart

About 2 pounds fish bones and heads
3–4 ribs celery, chunked
1 fennel bulb, cubed
2–3 leeks, cubed
1 bay leaf
1 thyme sprig
2–3 parsley stalks
$\frac{1}{4}$ teaspoon white peppercorns
$\frac{1}{2}$ teaspoon sea salt

1 Rinse the fish bones and heads and pack them into a large stockpot. Cover with 2 quarts water. Bring to a rolling boil and skim off the gray foam that rises to the surface.

2 Add the remaining ingredients and bubble up again. Turn down the heat and simmer for 30 minutes—no longer or the stock will taste bitter.

3 Strain out the solids and return the stock to the pan. Bubble up until reduced by half, making a well-flavored stock. Keep in the refrigerator in a covered container for no longer than two days, or freeze in ice cube trays and store for no longer than one month.

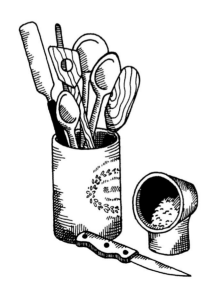

Beef Stock

Makes about 1½ quarts

4 pounds beef bones, sawn into
  short lengths
1 chicken carcass (bones only) or
  1 pound chicken wings and necks
2–3 large carrots, cubed
1 pound leeks, cubed
2 large onions, unskinned
  and quartered
2–3 ribs celery, cubed
1 bay leaf
4 parsley sprigs
1 thyme sprig
½ teaspoon peppercorns
Salt

Tip

A beef stock is
particularly suitable for
robust main course soups
such as Austria's rindsuppe
and France's pot-au-feu.

1 Preheat the oven to 350°F. Spread the beef bones on a large baking sheet or roasting pan and transfer to the oven until well-browned—allow 30 minutes. This preliminary roasting is essential to flavor as well as color the finished stock.

2 Pack the roasted bones in a large stockpot with the remaining ingredients. Add 3 quarts of water. Bring the water gently to a boil, allow one big belch, and reduce the heat to a simmer. Cover loosely and leave to cook gently—the surface should tremble, no more—for 2 hours or so, until the stock is well flavored and reduced by half.

3 Strain the stock, discarding the solids. Leave the broth to cool.

4 Lift off the layer of creamy fat (save it for roast potatoes). Store the stock in the refrigerator in a covered container for no longer than 1 week. To keep it for longer, freeze it in ice cube trays and use within 3 months.

Ham or Bacon Stock

Makes about 1½ quarts

1 ham hock or bacon hock
2–3 onions, cubed
2–3 large carrots, cubed
1 celeriac root, cubed
About a thumb's length parsley root
   (or 4–5 parsley stalks)
1 bay leaf
6–8 allspice berries
½ teaspoon peppercorns
Small bunch of dill and small bunch
   of savory (optional)

1 Put the ham hock or bacon hock in a large stockpot with all the other ingredients and 3 quarts of cold water. Bring to a boil, skim off the gray foam, and add a spoonful of cold water to send the cloudy pieces to the bottom. Repeat this process twice more.

2 Simmer gently for about 1½ hours, or until the stock is well flavored and reduced by half. It won't need extra salt.

3 Strain the stock, discard the solids, and allow the stock to cool. Lift off the layer of creamy fat.

4 Store in the refrigerator in a covered container for no more than 1 week. To keep it for longer, freeze in ice cube trays and use within 3 months.

Tip
A stock made with a ham or bacon hock is particularly good for winter soups—such as cabbage or potato. If the meat is salty, bring it to a boil in enough water to cover, then drain, discard the water, and start again with fresh water.

Dashi Stock

Makes about 1 quart

About 4 inches dried kombu (kelp)
2 tablespoons katsuo (dried bonito flakes)

1 Put the kombu in a saucepan with 1 quart of cold water and bring it very gently to a boil—the process should take about 10 minutes.

2 Remove the kombu and add 4 tablespoons of cold water. Stir in the katsuo and return the broth to a boil. Remove from the heat and allow to cool.

3 Strain and use as required.

- *Clear Beet Consommé*

- *Beef Consommé*

- *Chicken Consommé*

- *Lobster Consommé*

- *Consommé à L'indienne*

- *Japanese Miso Soup
  with Shiitake Mushrooms*

- *Vietnamese Chicken Broth
  with Lemon Grass & Ginger*

- *Consommé Madrilène*

- *Spanish Fifteen-Minute Soup*

- *Chinese Egg-Flower Soup*

CHAPTER ONE

CONSOMMÉS & CLEAR SOUPS

Clear Beet Consommé

Serves 4–6

1 quart beef or chicken consommé
   (see pp.24 & 25)
1 large beet, cooked and grated
²/₃ cup thick, drained yogurt
   (Greek style)
A few dill sprigs

1 Heat the consommé with the grated beet in a saucepan and remove the pan from the heat as soon as it boils.

2 Strain, discarding the beet which should have tinted the soup a deep ruby pink.

3 Reheat the consommé and ladle into small bowls. Drop a spoonful of yogurt into each bowl and finish with a sprig of dill.

Tip

This is a great little summer soup—full of vitamins and low in fat. If you fancy a slightly sharper flavor, add a dash of vinegar and lemon juice.

Beef Consommé

Serves 4–6

2 pounds lean beef shin, chopped

2 large onions, unskinned and chopped

2 large carrots, chopped

2 quarts strained beef stock (see p.17)

1 tablespoon chopped tomato flesh, if necessary

3 egg whites, well whisked

Tip

A crystal clear beef consommé is one of the simplest and most delicious of starters.

1 Put the beef in a large saucepan with the onions, carrots, and stock. Bring to a boil and leave to simmer gently for 2 hours, or until the meat has given up all its goodness and the broth has reduced by half. If the color is not sufficiently golden, you may add a tablespoon of chopped tomato flesh.

2 Strain the broth, discarding the vegetables and meat (or save it for a beef salad), and return the broth to the pan.

3 Bring the broth back to a boil and whisk in the egg whites. Return to a boil, reduce the heat, and simmer for 20 minutes, or until the egg whites float to the top, collecting all the impurities on the way.

4 Remove the pan from the heat and strain the broth through a strainer lined with a clean cloth. Blot the surface with paper towels to remove any lingering bubbles of fat.

5 Reheat, taste, and adjust the seasoning. Ladle into double-handled consommé bowls— very French.

• Good with Cheese Straws (see p.239).

Chicken Consommé

Serves 4–6

2 pounds chicken joints (drumsticks
or wings)
2 onions, chopped
4–5 ribs celery, chopped
2 quarts strained chicken stock
(see p.15)
1 strip lemon zest
1–2 tarragon sprigs
3 egg whites, well whisked

1 Rinse the chicken joints and pack them into a large saucepan with the onions, celery, and stock. Bring to a boil and allow to simmer gently for 2 hours, or until the chicken has given up all its goodness and the broth has reduced by half.

2 Add the lemon zest and tarragon and leave to infuse on the side of the cooker for 10 minutes. Strain the broth, discarding the solids.

3 Return the broth to the pan, bring it back to a boil, and whisk in the egg whites. Return to a boil, reduce the heat, and simmer for 20 minutes, or until the egg white floats to the top, collecting the impurities on the way.

4 Remove the pan from the heat and strain the broth through a strainer lined with a clean cloth. Blot the surface with paper towels to remove any lingering bubbles of fat.

5 To serve, reheat until just boiling, taste, and add salt.

• Good with crisp Melba Toast (see p.248).

Lobster Consommé

Serves 4–6

1½ quarts fish stock (see p.16)
Debris of 2–3 large lobsters (shells, heads, and legs)
1 cup dry white wine
1 red bell pepper, seeded and diced
2 tablespoons diced tomato
1 small fennel bulb, chopped
1 strip of orange zest
2 egg whites, whisked
Meat from 1 lobster claw or
   1 tablespoon peeled, cooked
   shrimps, to serve (optional)

1 Put the fish stock, lobster debris, white wine, red pepper, tomato, fennel, and orange zest in a large saucepan. Bring to a boil and bubble up. Allow one big belch, reduce the heat to low, and simmer gently for 30 minutes, or until the alcohol has evaporated and the volume is reduced by about half.

2 Strain the broth, discarding the solids, and return it to the pan. Bring back to a boil, stir in the whisked egg whites, and return to a boil. Reduce the heat and simmer for 10 minutes, or until the egg whites are floating on the surface and have gathered up all the remaining debris.

3 Strain the broth through a strainer lined with a clean cloth. Serve in double-handled consommé cups ladled over a slice or two of lobster claw meat or peeled shrimps, if you like.

• Good with Garlic Bread (see p.243).

Consommé à L'indienne

Serves 4–6

2 cups beef consommé (see p.24)
2–3 cardamom pods, toasted
   and crushed
1–2 small dried chiles

To finish
$\frac{2}{3}$ cup heavy cream, whipped
1 teaspoon curry powder

1 Bring the consommé to a boil in a large saucepan with the cardamom pods and chiles. Remove from the heat and leave to infuse for 10 minutes.

2 Strain, ladle into small soup bowls, and top each serving with a spoonful of whipped cream and a pinch of curry powder. Simple but surprisingly good, particularly with poppadoms on the side.

Japanese Miso Soup
with Shiitake Mushrooms

Serves 4–6

1 quart dashi stock (see p.19)
¼ cup dried shiitake mushrooms,
  soaked in hot water for 30 minutes
  to swell
5 tablespoons miso paste
2 tablespoons dried wakame
  (seaweed) flakes

To finish
1–2 cilantro sprigs, leaves only

1 Heat the dashi stock in a large saucepan until boiling. Meanwhile, drain the shiitake mushrooms, remove, and discard the tough stalks and slice the caps.

2 As soon as the stock boils, remove a ladleful and stir it into the miso paste, mixing until well blended, and then stir it back into the stock.

3 Return the stock to a boil, add the mushrooms and wakame flakes, and simmer gently for 10–15 minutes, or until the mushrooms are tender and the soup has taken their flavor.

4 Ladle into warm bowls (Japanese soup bowls are lidded for extra drama when serving), garnishing each portion with cilantro leaves.

Vietnamese Chicken Broth

with Lemon Grass & Ginger

Serves 4–6

1 quart chicken stock (see p.15)
1 lemon grass stalk, trimmed
  and chopped
1 slice fresh root ginger, shredded
2 tablespoons cellophane noodles

To finish
2–3 cilantro sprigs, leaves only
1 green chile, seeded and thinly sliced
Quartered limes

1 Bring the chicken stock to a boil in a large saucepan with the lemon grass and ginger. Remove from the heat and leave to infuse for 20 minutes.

2 Meanwhile, soak the noodles in warm water for 15 minutes to swell.

3 Strain the flavored broth, discarding the lemon grass and ginger. Return the broth to the pan and reheat until boiling. Add the noodles, bring back to a boil, and simmer for 5 minutes.

4 Ladle the soup and noodles into small soup bowls and finish each portion with a few cilantro leaves and sliced green chile. Serve with quartered limes for squeezing.

Consommé Madrilène

Serves 4–6

3–4 large ripe tomatoes, halved
2 red bell peppers, seeded and sliced
1 quart beef consommé (see p.24)

To finish
1 tomato, skinned, seeded, and diced

Tip
If you want to give this soup an extra kick, try adding a splash of dry sherry and a tablespoon of pimiento.

1 Preheat the oven to 350°F. Arrange the tomatoes and peppers on a non-stick baking sheet and roast for 20–30 minutes, or until the tomato flesh has collapsed and the pepper is soft and a little browned.

2 Heat the consommé with the tomatoes and peppers in a saucepan, but remove from the heat just before it boils. Infuse for 20 minutes, or until the consommé is a rich, deep red and the sediment has settled on the bottom of the pan.

3 Pour the consommé off the sediment (you may need to strain it as well). Return the consommé to a boil. Drop a few pieces of diced tomato into each serving bowl and pour the boiling consommé over the top. Serve.

• Good with Catalan Bread and Tomato (see p.245).

Spanish Fifteen-Minute Soup

Serves 4–6

1 quart chicken, beef, or ham stock
(see pp.15, 17 & 18)
2 tablespoons diced serrano ham
2 tablespoons vermicelli or angel-hair
pasta
2 hard-boiled eggs, diced
1 tablespoon fresh chopped parsley
1 tablespoon fresh chopped mint

1 Bring the chicken, beef, or ham stock to a boil in a saucepan with the diced serrano ham. Reduce the heat and simmer for 10 minutes.

2 Add the vermicelli or angel-hair pasta, stir, return to a boil, and simmer for 3–4 minutes, or until the pasta is soft.

3 Remove from the heat and stir in the chopped eggs, parsley, and mint. Ladle into soup bowls.

Chinese Egg-Flower Soup

Serves 4–6

1 quart clear chicken stock
  (see p.15)
1 slice fresh root ginger, pressed to
  extract the juice
2 tablespoons Chinese rice wine or
  dry sherry
1 teaspoon sesame oil
2 large eggs, lightly beaten to blend
2–3 scallions, trimmed and
  sliced diagonally, to garnish

1 In a medium saucepan, bring the stock gently to a boil with the ginger juice, rice wine, or sherry and sesame oil.

2 Using a pair of chopsticks or a slotted spoon, swirl the stock in a clockwise direction and pour in the beaten egg. Immediately remove from the heat and swirl the soup in the opposite direction so that the egg makes a flowery pattern.

3 Ladle into soup bowls and finish each portion with a sprinkling of sliced scallion.

• Good with Sizzling Rice Crisps (see p.249).

Tip

To create perfect strands of egg in your soup, try slowly streaming the beaten egg through a fork about 8 inches above the soup. This method ensures that the egg streams in very slowly, and the size of the fork tines give the strands the perfect thickness.

CHILLED SOUPS

- Gazpacho
- Chilled Celery Soup with Lemon Gremolata
- Cold Almond Soup
- Chilled Sorrel Soup
- Chilled Watercress Soup
- Chilled Asparagus Soup
- Chilled Avocado Soup
- Vichyssoise
- Cold Almond & Chicken Velouté
- Chilled Yogurt Soup with Cucumber, Walnuts & Dill
- Chilled Tarragon Soup
- Chilled Tomato Cream with Fresh Basil
- Chilled Red Pepper Soup

CHAPTER TWO

CHILLED SOUPS

Gazpacho

Serves 4–6

1 slice day-old bread
2 tablespoons white wine vinegar
2 cloves garlic, crushed
2 tablespoons olive oil
1 small cucumber, or ½ large one, peeled and roughly chopped
2 pounds tomatoes, skinned, seeded, and chopped
1 green bell pepper, seeded and diced
About 3 cups iced water
Sugar, to taste
Salt

Optional extras
Hot croûtons (diced bread fried in a little olive oil)
Chopped hard-boiled egg
Diced serrano ham
Diced cucumber
Diced bell peppers
Tomato, skinned and diced
Mild onion, chopped

1 Tear the bread into small pieces. Place the bread pieces into a bowl containing 2 tablespoons of water, the vinegar, and garlic and allow to soak for 10 minutes.

2 Transfer the bread and its soaking liquid to a food processor or blender. Add all the remaining ingredients except for the seasoning and process everything until smooth.

3 Add 1 cup of water until you have the consistency you like, thick or thin, depending on whether you wish to serve your gazpacho as a refreshment or a soup. Adjust the seasoning with salt and a little sugar.

4 Transfer the gazpacho to a jug and cover securely. Set in a cold larder or the refrigerator for 2–3 hours, or until well chilled.

5 As a refreshment, serve the gazpacho in long, chilled glasses. As a first-course soup, ladle into bowls and hand round the extras separately for people to add their own.

Note: the color of gazpacho is dependent on the ripeness of your tomatoes. For a warmer pink color chose very ripe tomatoes.

Chilled Celery Soup
with Lemon Gremolata

Serves 4-6

1 small celery head (green unblanched
    for preference)
1 tablespoon olive oil
1 onion, diced small
1 large potato, peeled and diced
3 cups water
1 bay leaf
1⅓ cups whole milk
Salt and pepper

To finish
1 tablespoon parsley leaves
1 clove garlic, crushed
1 tablespoon finely-grated lemon zest

1 Rinse and chop the celery stalks, reserving the heart.

2 Heat the olive oil in a medium saucepan and add the chopped onion. Fry gently until it softens—don't let it take color. Add the diced potato and the chopped celery stalks, and continue to fry gently, loosely lidded, for 5 minutes. Add water, bring to the boil, add salt and pepper, turn down the heat, and simmer for 10-15 minutes, until the vegetables are perfectly tender. Process the soup and the milk till smooth. Taste and adjust the seasoning. Chill.

3 Meanwhile, prepare the gremolata: chop the reserved celery heart, parsley, garlic, and lemon zest together until well-blended.

4 Ladle the soup into bowls and finish each portion with gremolata. Perfect with focaccia hot from the oven.

Cold Almond Soup

Serves 4–6

2 tablespoons blanched almonds
4 cloves garlic, roughly chopped
About 3 cups iced water
2 tablespoons olive oil
About 2 tablespoons white
    wine vinegar
2 tablespoons fresh white
    bread crumbs
Salt

To finish
12–18 small green grapes, peeled
    and seeded

Tip
Cold Almond Soup is a variation of the classic Spanish Gazpacho. Also known as White Gazpacho, it originates from Andalusia.

1 Put the almonds and garlic in food processor or blender with just enough of the water to keep the blades turning. Process to a paste.

2 Add half the remaining water, the oil, vinegar, and bread crumbs and process thoroughly until smooth. Add the remaining water until you have the consistency you like.

3 Season with salt (check if you need a little more vinegar). Transfer to the refrigerator for an hour or so, or until well chilled.

4 Serve in small cups, bowls or glasses, depending on how diluted you have decided it should be. Float 3 or 4 grapes on top of each serving—don't worry if they drop to the bottom.

• Serve with hot Croûtons fried in olive oil (see p.224).

Chilled Sorrel Soup

Serves 4

2 generous handfuls sorrel leaves, rinsed and shredded
$\frac{1}{4}$ stick (2 tablespoons) butter
3 cups strong chicken stock (see p.15)
1 tablespoon all-purpose flour
$\frac{1}{2}$ cup heavy cream
Salt and ground black pepper

To finish
A little more heavy cream
A few sorrel leaves, shredded

1 Drop the sorrel in a saucepan with a pinch of salt and the butter, cover tightly, and shake over the heat for 2–3 minutes, or until the leaves collapse.

2 Drop the contents of the pan into a food processor or blender with the chicken stock and the flour and process until smooth. Alternatively, finely chop the sorrel, blend with the flour, and add the stock.

3 Tip everything back into the pan and bring to a boil, whisking until it thickens a little and no longer tastes of raw flour. Whisk in the cream. Check the seasoning and add salt and pepper to taste. Remove the pan from the heat and leave to cool.

4 Serve chilled, with a swirl of cream and the shredded sorrel. Serve with hot crusty rolls and unsalted butter.

Chilled Watercress Soup

Serves 4–6

1 large bunch (about 1 cup) watercress
1 large leek, including the green,
  thinly sliced
1 large potato, cubed
3 cups vegetable or chicken stock
  (see pp.14 & 15)
1 cup light cream
1 tablespoon lemon juice
Salt and ground black pepper

1 Rinse the watercress and strip the leaves from the stalks, reserving both in separate piles.

2 Put the leek, potato, and watercress stalks in a medium saucepan with the vegetable or chicken stock and 1 teaspoon salt. Bring to a boil, turn down the heat, and simmer gently for about 30 minutes, until the potato is tender enough to collapse into the broth.

3 Transfer the contents of the pan to a food processor or blender. Process until smooth, or push through a strainer. Let cool.

4 Add the cream (saving a spoonful for finishing), the lemon juice, and all but a few of the watercress leaves. Process again until the soup is pale green and well flavored with watercress. Taste, and add salt and freshly ground pepper. Chill in the refrigerator for 1–2 hours.

5 Finish the soup with the reserved watercress leaves and an extra swirl of cream.

• Good served with Garlic Bread (see p.243).

Chilled Asparagus Soup

Serves 4–6

1 pound green asparagus, trimmed
1 cup potatoes, diced
3–4 scallions, diced
1 bay leaf
2 cups vegetable or chicken stock
  (see pp.14 & 15)
1 cup half and half
Salt and ground black pepper

To finish
¹⁄₂ cup sour cream

1 Chop the asparagus into short lengths, reserving the tips.

2 Put the asparagus, potatoes, scallions, and bay leaf into a large saucepan with the stock. Bring to a boil, cover, and reduce the heat. Cook for 20 minutes, or until the potatoes are soft.

3 Push everything through a strainer to remove the stringy stalks. Transfer to a food processor or blender with the cream and process until smooth. Season with salt and pepper. Allow to cool, then transfer to the refrigerator to chill.

4 When you are ready to serve, drop the asparagus tips in boiling salted water for 2-3 minutes—just long enough to take the edge off their crispness. Remove with a slotted spoon and pass them under the cold tap to keep them fresh and green.

5 Ladle the soup into bowls and finish each serving with a swirl of sour cream and a few asparagus tips.

Chilled Avocado Soup

Serves 4–6

2 ripe avocados
$1/2$ cucumber, peeled and diced
1 green bell pepper, cored and seeded
$1/2$ mild onion, chopped
1 clove garlic, chopped
1 green chile, seeded and sliced
Juice of 2 limes (or lemons)
$1^{1}/2$ cups ice-cold water
1 teaspoon salt
Small bunch of fresh cilantro
Salt

To serve
Quartered limes
Coarse sea salt
Tortilla chips (see p.247)

1 Halve, stone, and skin the avocados. Drop the flesh of the avocados into a food processor or blender with the cucumber, green pepper, onion, garlic, chile, and lime juice. Add $1^{1}/2$ cups ice-cold water and 1 teaspoon salt. Process thoroughly until smooth.

2 Add a handful of fresh cilantro leaves and another $1^{1}/2$ cups cold water, and process briefly—just long enough to chop the cilantro, which should still be visible as little flecks. Taste and adjust the seasoning, remembering that you will be handing round more salt with the lime quarters for people to add their own. Serve chilled and with lime quarters, coarse sea salt, and tortilla chips separately.

Tip
For a Mexican splash, accompany with little glasses of chilled Tequila, either to sip with a suck of lime and a lick of salt, or to stir directly into the soup.

Vichyssoise

Serves 4–6

2 large leeks, white part only,
   thinly sliced
2 large potatoes, chunked
Bouquet garni (bay leaf, thyme, and
   parsley, tied in a bunch)
²/₃ cup half and half
Salt and ground black pepper

To finish
Chopped chives

1 Put the vegetables in a large saucepan with just enough water to cover—about 3½ cups. Add the bouquet garni and a little salt. Bring to a boil and simmer for 30-40 minutes, or until the potatoes are perfectly soft.

2 Remove the bouquet garni. Put everything in a food processor or blender and process until smooth. (For a thinner, more delicate puree, push the vegetables through a strainer.)

3 Add the cream and process until well blended. Taste and season generously with salt and pepper. Allow to cool and transfer to the refrigerator to chill. Finish with a sprinkling of chives.

• Good with radishes and hot, buttery Garlic Bread (see p.243).

Chilled Almond
& Chicken Velouté

Serves 4–6

½ cup blanched almonds
2 cups chicken stock (see p.15)
1⅓ cups half and half
2 egg yolks

To finish
Half and half
Toasted flaked almonds

Tip
Freshly-ground almonds add a subtle layer of flavor and texture to a classic French velouté.

1 Put the almonds in a food processor or blender with enough chicken stock to allow the blades to revolve freely, and process the almonds to a paste. Add the rest of the ingredients and continue to process until smooth.

2 Transfer the contents of the processor to a heavy saucepan. Heat gently without allowing the soup to boil, stirring continuously until the liquid thickens slightly—don't let it overcook. Cool and transfer to the refrigerator to chill.

3 Finish with an extra swirl of half and half and a few toasted almond flakes.

- Good with Cheese Straws (see p.239).

Chilled Yogurt Soup
with Cucumber, Walnuts & Dill

Serves 4–6

3 cups unflavored yogurt
2 tablespoons shelled walnuts
1 small cucumber or half a large
   one, grated
2–3 cloves garlic, grated
1 small bunch of dill, leaves only

1 Grate the cucumber and sprinkle with salt.
Leave to drain in a colander for half an hour.

2 Whisk the yogurt with 4 tablespoons cold
water until well blended.

3 Wrap the walnuts in a clean cloth and crush
them with a rolling pin.

4 Rinse the cucumber and stir into the yogurt
with the crushed walnuts, garlic, and dill.

5 Transfer to the refrigerator until you are ready
to serve.

• Good with fingers of Pita Bread (see p.242) fried
until crisp in a little olive oil.

Chilled Tarragon Soup

Serves 4–6

1 large handful fresh tarragon leaves
   (at least ¼ cup, keep stalks
   separately)
1 tablespoon finely chopped onion
1 tablespoon unsalted butter
1 tablespoon all-purpose flour
3 cups vegetable or chicken stock
   (see pp.14 & 15)
1 cup white wine
2 egg yolks
½ cup sour cream
½ cup fresh spinach leaves, shredded
Salt and ground black pepper
Tarragon sprigs, to garnish

1 Shred the tarragon leaves finely and reserve. Tie the stalks in a little bunch.

2 Fry the onion gently in the butter in a saucepan. As soon as the onion softens, stir in the flour and fry for another 2–3 minutes—don't let anything brown. Without removing the pan from the heat, gradually whisk in the stock, beating to avoid lumps. As soon as it boils, add the wine, bubble up, reduce the heat, and cook until the alcohol has evaporated and the steam no longer smells of wine.

3 Add the bunch of tarragon stalks, reduce the heat, and simmer gently for 10 minutes to cook the flour and marry the flavors.

4 Meanwhile, whisk the egg yolks with the sour cream until well blended, then whisk in a ladleful of the hot soup. Remove the pan from the heat, discard the tarragon stalks, then whisk in the egg and cream mixture, blending until smooth. Stir in the shredded tarragon and spinach leaves. Taste and adjust the seasoning. Allow to cool before transferring to the refrigerator to chill.

5 Ladle into soup bowls and finish each serving with a sprig of tarragon.

• Good with hot Salt Crackers (see p.240).

Chilled Tomato Cream

with Fresh Basil

Serves 4–6

3 cups tomato juice
1⅓ cups light cream
1 teaspoon sugar
2–3 drops Tabasco or chili sauce

To finish
3–4 basil sprigs, leaves only
1 tablespoon grated lemon zest

1 Combine the tomato juice with the cream in a food processor or blender. Add the sugar and a few drops of Tabasco or chili sauce and chill in the refrigerator for a couple of hours.

2 Top with shredded basil leaves and grated lemon zest.

• Good with Parmesan Crisps (see p.249).

Chilled Red Pepper Soup

Serves 4–6

1 large onion, thinly sliced
2 tablespoons olive oil
3–4 ripe red bell peppers (about
   1 pound)
3 cups vegetable, chicken, or beef
   stock (see pp.14, 15 & 17)
About 1 tablespoon sherry or white
   wine vinegar
$1/2$ teaspoon hot pimentón (Spanish
   paprika) or chili powder
About 1 teaspoon sugar
Salt

To finish
Fresh marjoram leaves

1 Fry the onion gently in the oil in a heavy saucepan until soft and golden—don't let it brown. This will take at least 15 minutes.

2 Meanwhile, roast the peppers by holding them on the end of a knife in a flame, turning them until the skin blackens and blisters. Alternatively, roast them in a very hot oven 450°F. Pop the hot peppers in a plastic bag, seal and leave for 10 minutes to allow the steam to loosen the skins. Cut the peppers in half, remove the seeds and carefully scrape the flesh from the skins in long strips.

3 Save a few pepper strips for garnish, and add the remaining pepper flesh to the onion in the pan. Add the stock, bubble up, and cook for 10 minutes to marry the flavors.

4 Transfer the contents of the pan to a food processor or blender, add the vinegar, pimentón or chili, and process until smooth. Season with the sugar and a little salt.

5 Allow to cool before transferring to the refrigerator to chill. Check the seasoning before serving the soup—you might need a little more vinegar, salt, or sugar.

6 Finish with the reserved pepper strips and a few marjoram leaves. Serve with toasted country bread topped with salt-cured anchovies and a little olive oil.

SEAFOOD SOUPS

- Shrimp Bisque
- Scottish Partan Bree
- Lobster or Crayfish Bisque
- Portuguese Fish Soup
- Mr Pickwick's Oyster Soup
- Spanish Shellfish Soup with Sherry
- Scottish Haddock & Potato Soup
- New England Clam Chowder
- Breton Chowder
- Bahamian Chowder
- Brittany Fish Soup
- Bergen Fish Soup
- Cambodian Hot-and-Sour Fish Soup
- Bouillabaisse
- Shrimp & Coconut Soup with Rice Noodles
- Portuguese Fisherman's Stew
- Greek Fish Soup
- Fish Soup with Paprika
- Catalan Fish Soup
- Fish Soup with Saffron
- Mussel Soup
- Scottish Tweed Kettle

CHAPTER THREE

SEAFOOD
SOUPS

Shrimp Bisque

Serves 4–6

1 cup raw shrimps
4 cups fish stock (see p.16)
¼ stick (2 tablespoons) unsalted butter
2 tablespoons all-purpose flour
1 teaspoon paprika
About 6 tablespoons heavy cream
3 egg yolks
Freshly grated nutmeg
Salt and freshly ground black pepper

Tip

A bisque is a rich thick soup usually made of pureed seafood most popularly lobster and crayfish (see p.59).

1 Shell the shrimps. Heat the stock in a saucepan with the shrimp debris and simmer for 15–20 minutes. Strain the broth and reserve.

2 Melt the butter in a roomy saucepan, stir in the flour, and fry until it turns a sandy color—don't let it brown. Sprinkle in the paprika and remove from the heat. Gradually add the strained broth and whisk over a gentle heat until it thickens.

3 Remove the pan from the heat and whisk in the cream and egg yolks. (You can do this in a food processor or blender if you like).

4 Reheat gently, whisking all the while, until the soup is just below boiling point. Taste and season with nutmeg, salt, and pepper.

5 Slip the shrimps into the soup and reheat until just below boiling point. Split between the bowls, making sure everyone gets their share of shrimps.

Scottish Partan Bree

Serves 4–6

About 2 dozen live swimmer crabs
  or 1 large cooked crab (with
  cooking water)
Large pat of butter
1 medium onion, quartered
2 ribs celery, chopped
1 medium carrot, chunked
1 medium tomato, chopped
$\frac{1}{2}$ teaspoon crushed black peppercorns
4 tablespoons ginger wine or
  oloroso sherry
Small bouquet garni (bay leaf, thyme,
  parsley, tied in a bunch)
Salt

To finish
2 egg yolks
4 tablespoons heavy cream
1 teaspoon paprika

1 If you are using swimmers, put the crabs in a bucket of fresh water and wait until they stop scuttling—they're seawater swimmers so fresh water sends them to sleep. Melt the butter in a roomy saucepan. When it foams, gently fry the onion, celery, and carrot until soft. Add the tomato and increase the heat, stirring until it softens. Then add 1 quart water (or crab cooking water), season with salt and the peppercorns, and bring to a boil.

2 If you are using swimmers, drain them and drop them straight into the boiling saucepan—don't worry, the heat will kill them instantly. If using cooked crab, remove the meat from the shell and add the debris to the pan, reserving the meat.

3 Bring the pan back to a boil and add the wine or sherry and the bouquet garni. Return the pan to a boil, cover loosely, reduce the heat, and leave to simmer for about 40 minutes, or until the broth has reduced by a third.

4 Remove the pan from the heat and allow to cool a little. If using swimmers, transfer everything to a food processor or blender, process thoroughly, then pour back into the pan through a strainer. If using a large crab, strain to remove the crab debris before processing and stir the reserved crab meat into the broth. This will leave you with a dense, fragrant, cloudy broth. Reheat gently until just below boiling point. Meanwhile, whisk the egg yolks with the cream and paprika, then whisk in a ladleful of the nearly boiling broth. Stir the egg mixture back into the broth, then stir over a low heat for a minute or two until it thickens a little. Check the seasoning and serve without reboiling.

Lobster or Crayfish Bisque

Serves 4–6

6 lobster or crayfish shells, including
   all the debris
1 tablespoon sunflower oil
1 large leek, chunked
1 carrot, chunked
1 small fennel bulb, quartered
$\frac{1}{2}$ teaspoon black peppercorns
2–3 parsley sprigs
3 cups fish stock (see p.16)
$\frac{2}{3}$ cup white wine
1 quart water

To finish
$\frac{1}{2}$ stick (4 tablespoons) unsalted butter
1 tablespoon all-purpose flour
$\frac{1}{2}$ cup heavy cream
1 teaspoon tomato paste
$\frac{1}{2}$ teaspoon paprika
Salt and ground white pepper
Lobster or crayfish meat (optional)

1 Preheat the oven to 450°F. Smash up the lobster or crayfish shells and spread all the debris in a roasting pan. Toss in the oil. Roast everything for 15–20 minutes, or until the shells and bits begin to brown—don't let anything burn.

2 Transfer the roasted debris to a large saucepan and add the leek, carrot, fennel (save the feathery greens), peppercorns, and parsley. Add the stock, wine, and water. Bring to a boil, reduce the heat, and leave to simmer very gently for 1 hour.

3 Strain the broth, pressing well to extract all the flavor, and return the stock to the pan. Bring it back to a boil and bubble up until you have 3 cups of well flavored broth.

4 Meanwhile, cream the butter with the flour until well blended. Stir it into the hot broth and whisk over the heat for about 5-6 minutes, until the soup thickens a little and no longer tastes of raw flour.

5 Whisk in the cream, tomato paste, and paprika. Taste and add salt and freshly ground white pepper. Finish with the reserved fennel green, finely chopped, and the lobster or crayfish meat, if available.

Portuguese Fish Soup

Serves 4–6

4½ pounds small bony fish (or the
   bones and heads of larger fish)
⅓ cup olive oil
2 medium onions, sliced
3–4 cloves garlic, chopped
1 red pepper, seeded and diced
1 large tomato, skinned and diced
   (or 1 tablespoon tomato paste)
1–2 bay leaves
1⅓ cups light red wine
1 pound yellow fleshed potatoes, sliced

To finish (optional)
A handful of squid rings or
   shelled shrimps

1 Rinse the fish or fish heads and bones, salt them lightly, and reserve.

2 Heat the olive oil in a roomy saucepan. Fry the onions and garlic very gently for 15 minutes or so, until soft and golden—don't let them brown. Add the diced pepper and fry for another 5 minutes.

3 Add the tomato flesh or paste and bubble up for a minute until it collapses. Add the bay leaf and wine and bubble up again until the alcohol has evaporated.

4 Add 1 quart cold water, bring to a boil, and add the fish or heads and bones. Bring back to a boil, turn down the heat, and simmer for 20-30 minutes, or until the fish is mushy.

5 Push everything through a strainer (or you can process it, but you will still have to strain it). Return the broth to the pan and bring back to a boil. Add the potatoes and simmer gently for 15-20 minutes, or until the potato is perfectly soft.

6 Add the optional squid rings or shrimps and reheat (if raw, wait until they turn opaque). Serve in deep bowls, with rough country bread.

Mr Pickwick's

Oyster Soup

Serves 4–6

12–18 oysters in the shell
2 cups fish stock (see p.16)
2 shallots or 1 small onion,
   finely chopped
$\frac{1}{2}$ cup white wine
1 bay leaf
2–3 parsley stalks
$\frac{1}{4}$ stick (2 tablespoons) unsalted butter
1 tablespoon all-purpose flour
1 cup heavy cream
1 teaspoon Worcestershire sauce
2–3 drops Tabasco sauce, plus
   extra to serve
Salt

To finish
Chopped onion, chives, or parsley

1 Hold each oyster over a fine strainer set over a bowl to catch the juices. With the oyster rounded shell up, insert the tip of an oyster knife, or short, strong-bladed knife, into the hinge. Twist the knife to prise the hinge open and cut the muscles above and below the oyster. Cut between the shells to open them and cut away the oyster with a knife.

2 Bring the stock to a boil in a large saucepan, and add the shallots or onion. Add the wine, bay leaf, and parsley stalks and bubble up until the steam no longer smells of alcohol, about 10 minutes. Remove the bay leaf and parsley stalks.

3 Cream the butter with the flour and stir it into the hot broth. Whisk until smooth. Stir in the cream and the reserved oyster juices and bubble up again. Season with the Worcestershire sauce and Tabasco, taste and add salt.

4 Slip the oysters into the hot soup and return to just below boiling point. Ladle into bowls, dividing the oysters between each serving.

5 Finish with a sprinkle of chopped raw onion, chives, or parsley. Hand round more Tabasco sauce for anyone who likes their oysters peppery.

- Good with warm Oatcakes (see p.246).

Spanish Shellfish Soup
with Sherry

Serves 4–6

2¼ pounds live shellfish (bivalves—
   clams, mussels)
1 tablespoon olive oil
1–2 cloves garlic, slivered
2 tablespoons finely diced serrano
   ham or bacon
½ teaspoon saffron (about 12 threads),
   toasted in a dry pan
1 tablespoon pimentón (Spanish
   paprika) or 1 Ñora (dried red
   pepper), seeded and torn
1 cup sherry (manzanilla or fino)
3 cups fish stock (see p.16)
Salt and ground black pepper

To finish
Chopped fresh flat leaf parsley
Quartered lemons

1 Put the shellfish to soak in cold water to spit
out their sand—overnight is best but 3–4 hours
will do. Drain and rinse thoroughly. Scrape the
beards from the mussels, if using.

2 Warm the olive oil in a large saucepan, add the
garlic and ham or bacon, and fry for a moment
until the garlic softens. Sprinkle with the saffron
and the pimentón or Ñora. Stir over the heat for
1 minute, then add the sherry and bubble up for
2–3 minutes, or until the steam no longer smells
of alcohol. Add the stock and bring to a boil.

3 Add the shellfish to the pan. Return to a
boil, cover and cook for 3–4 minutes until
the shellfish open. Discard any that remain closed.
Remove the pan from the heat, taste, and adjust
the seasoning.

4 Garnish with chopped parsley and serve
without reheating, with quartered lemons and
bread for mopping. Provide a bowl for the debris.

Scottish Haddock

& Potato Soup

Serves 4–6

1 whole smoked haddock (about
   12 ounces)
2 leeks, thinly sliced
2$\frac{1}{4}$ pounds potatoes, sliced
3 cups whole milk
$\frac{1}{2}$ stick (4 tablespoons) unsalted butter,
   slivered
Chopped hard-boiled egg (optional)
Sea salt and ground black pepper

To finish
Chopped chives

Tip
You could use proper
smoked haddock on the
bone—pale honey-colored
whole fish split right down the
bone rather than the
bright yellow fillets. Smoked
salmon is a possible
alternative.

1 Put the haddock in a saucepan with enough water to cover. Bring to a boil, allow a big belch, then remove the haddock with a slotted spoon. Skin and bone the fish, reserving the flesh and discarding the rest. Flake the fish.

2 Put the leeks and potatoes in the pan with the cooking water, add the milk, and bring to a boil. Turn down the heat to a gentle simmer, season with salt and freshly ground pepper, and cook for 15–20 minutes, or until the potato is perfectly soft.

3 Stir in the reserved flaked fish and the butter and reheat until just below boiling point. Stir in the chopped hard-boiled egg, if using, and taste and adjust the seasoning.

4 Ladle into soup bowls and finish each portion with a sprinkle of chives.

New England Clam Chowder

Serves 4–6

2 dozen live clams (quahogs or
   steamers)
½ stick (4 tablespoons) butter, plus
   extra to serve
½ cup salt pork or unsmoked
   bacon, diced
2 onions, thinly sliced
1 pound waxy white-fleshed potatoes,
   diced or sliced
2 cups milk
1 pound cod fillet or other white fish
   fillet, skinned and diced
Salt and pepper

To finish
4–6 crackers (or matzos or water
   biscuits)
⅔ cup heavy cream

1 Rinse the clams, discarding any that don't
retract the neck or feeder-tube when touched.
Pop them in the freezer for 1–2 hours to make
them easier to open. Lever the shells apart with a
short, stout knife (do this over a bowl to catch the
juice) and slip the fish off their shells. Remove the
dark stomach, chop the meat and reserve.

2 Melt half the butter in a pan and fry the salt
pork or bacon and onions gently until soft and
golden—allow at least 10 minutes.

3 Add the potatoes and 1⅓ cups water. Bring to
a boil, turn down the heat, and cover loosely.
Simmer until the potatoes are nearly soft, about
10 minutes.

4 Add the milk and the reserved clam juice to
the pan, return to a boil, add the diced fish, and
poach for 2–3 minutes—just long enough for them
to turn opaque. Break in the crackers.

5 Add the chopped shellfish meat with its juices.
Heat everything together gently, stirring to
marry the flavors. Remove from the heat and stir in
the cream. Season to taste with salt and pepper.

6 Put a pat of butter into each soup dish before
you pour in the hot chowder. Serve with thick-
cut brown bread.

Breton Chowder

Serves 6–8

The fish (gutted and scaled but left whole)
2 medium mackerel
3 smallish mullets
1 pound halibut
2 haddock
1 small sea bream

The broth
1 tablespoon unsalted butter or
    pork lard
2 medium onions, chopped
2–3 cloves garlic, chopped
2¼ pounds potatoes, chopped into
    bite-sized pieces
1 cup soft-leaved herbs (chervil, sorrel,
    parsley, chives), shredded
Salt and ground black pepper

To finish
Baguette or any crusty French bread
Unsalted French butter, melted, or a
    vinaigrette made with Dijon mustard,
    olive oil and wine vinegar

1 Rinse the fish and chunk it into bite-sized pieces, discarding the heads if you feel you must. Salt lightly and set aside in a cool place.

2 For the broth, melt the butter or lard in a large saucepan. Add the onions and garlic and fry gently until softened and golden. Add 1 quart of water, bring to a boil, and add the potatoes and a little salt. Return to a boil, reduce the heat, and cover the pan. Simmer for 20 minutes, or until the potatoes are tender.

3 Stir in the shredded herbs and check the seasoning. Return to a boil and lay the chunked fish in the broth. Cover and cook for 3–4 minutes, or until the fish flesh has firmed and turned opaque—don't overcook it.

4 Serve the broth first, ladled into deep soup plates in which you have placed a slice or two of bread. Serve the fish and potatoes in the same plate with melted butter or a vinaigrette to moisten.

Bahamian Chowder

Serves 4–6

1¼ pounds fresh swordfish steaks,
  diced
1 pound fresh tuna steaks, diced
3 cups fish stock (see p.16)
1 pound tomatoes, skinned, seeded,
  and diced
1 tablespoon butter
6–8 allspice berries, roughly crushed
1–2 Scotch bonnet chiles, seeded
  and chopped (or ½ teaspoon dried
  chiles, torn)
1 pound sweet potato, diced
1 pound pumpkin, diced
Salt and freshly ground black pepper

To finish
Quartered limes or lemons
Tabasco or salsa piri-piri (see p.236)

1 Salt the fish lightly and set it aside.

2 Put the fish stock in a large saucepan and bring it to a boil.

3 Meanwhile, fry the tomatoes in the butter until the flesh collapses. Add the allspice and chiles and fry for another minute.

4 Tip the contents of the pan into the boiling fish stock, add the sweet potato and pumpkin, and return to a boil. Cover loosely and bubble up for 15–20 minutes, or until the vegetables are tender.

5 Slip in the fish, reheat, and simmer for 3–4 minutes, or until the flesh turns opaque —don't overcook it.

6 Taste and adjust the seasoning. Ladle into bowls and serve with quartered limes or lemons for squeezing, and Tabasco or piri-piri sauce on the side.

Brittany Fish Soup

Serves 4–6

About 1pound whole flatfish (such as
plaice, sole, halibut), cleaned

About 1 pound white fish (such as cod,
hake, haddock), cleaned

$\frac{1}{2}$ stick (4 tablespoons) unsalted butter

$\frac{1}{2}$ cup mushrooms (chanterelles,
if you can get them), diced

2 tablespoons Calvados or
apple brandy

1 cup apple cider

2 cups fish stock (see p.16)

$1\frac{1}{4}$ live mussels, scrubbed and bearded

1 tablespoon all-purpose flour creamed
with 1 tablespoon butter

$\frac{1}{2}$ cup heavy cream

2–3 tarragon sprigs or a handful
chervil, chopped

1 Prepare the fish as you please. Fillet or chop it, or leave it whole, depending on the size of the fish and your guests' preferences.

2 Melt the butter in a large saucepan and add the mushrooms and fish. Fry gently, turning the fish once, until lightly browned.

3 Pour the Calvados or brandy over the contents of the pan and light the alcohol with a match. Wait until the alcohol burns off, then add the cider and the stock.

4 Bring rapidly to a boil and gently place the mussels on top of the fish. Cover and wait for 5 minutes for the shells to open in the steam.

5 Transfer the fish and mussels to deep soup plates. Discard any mussels that remain closed.

6 Reheat the broth, stir in the creamed flour and butter, and bubble up for 3-4 minutes, whisking until the broth thickens a little. Stir in the cream and bubble up again. Stir in the herbs and ladle the creamy broth over the fish.

• Good with Croûtons fried in butter (see p.224).

Bergen Fish Soup

Serves 4

4 cod steaks (weighing about 4 ounces
   each) or 8 ounces raw jumbo prawns
   or 1 medium-sized cod roe (about
   12 ounces)
1 quart fish stock (see p.16)
1½ pounds potatoes, peeled and diced
1 medium onion, thinly sliced
1 thick slice ham, diced finely
¼ stick (2 tablespoons) butter
1 pound live mussels
2 egg yolks
2 tablespoons heavy cream
Salt and freshly ground black pepper

To finish
A few dill sprigs
1 tablespoon pickled onions, diced

1 Wipe over the cod steaks and salt them lightly.
Rinse the cod roe and wrap in a double
envelope of parchment paper. Bring a pan of salted
water to a boil and slip in the packet of roe. Bring
back to a boil and then turn down the heat. Simmer
until the roe is firm—a medium-sized roe takes
about 25 minutes. Leave it in the water to cool.
Unwrap and slice thickly.

2 In a large saucepan, bring the fish stock to a
boil with the potatoes. Turn down the heat
and cover loosely. Simmer for 10–15 minutes, or
until the potatoes are nearly tender. Meanwhile,
fry the onion and ham gently in the butter in a
small skillet until the onion is soft and golden.
Scrub and beard (remove the whiskery little tags
on the shell) the mussels.

3 Tip the contents of the skillet into the soup
and lay the mussels on top. Bring back to a
boil, cover, and cook for 5 minutes (just enough to
cook the prawns and open the mussels).

4 Carefully, with a slotted spoon, transfer the
solids to a warmed, deep soup tureen. Discard
any mussels that remain closed. Slip the cod steaks
into the broth and let them poach for 3–4 minutes,
or until firm, then transfer to the tureen.

5 Whisk the egg yolks with the cream. Whisk in
a ladleful of the boiling broth. Stir this back into
the soup and reheat gently—don't let it boil or the
egg will scramble. Taste and add salt and pepper.
Pour the soup over the fish, vegetables, and cod roe,
and sprinkle with chopped dill and a few diced
pickled onions.

Cambodian

Hot-and-Sour Fish Soup

Serves 4–6

2 cloves garlic, crushed
1 slice fresh root ginger, finely chopped
1 lemon grass stalk, chopped
1 quart fish stock (see p.16)
$\frac{1}{2}$ teaspoon salt
8 ounces white fish steaks
4 ounces vermicelli or other soup noodles
1–2 green chiles, seeded and thinly sliced
Juice of 1 lime

1 In a saucepan, simmer the garlic, ginger, and lemon grass in the fish stock for 20 minutes. Meanwhile, salt the fish lightly on both sides, cover with plastic wrap, and leave in a cool place while the stock cooks.

2 Strain the stock and return it to the pan. Bring back to a boil and add the fish steaks.

3 Return the soup to a boil and drop in the vermicelli or soup noodles. Bubble gently for 2-3 minutes, until the noodles are soft and the fish has turned opaque. Season with the chiles and the lime juice and serve.

Bouillabaisse

Serves 6–8

The fish (you need 6½ pounds of at least five different varieties, one of which must be a rockfish such as blackfish). Choose from:
Sea bass
Monkfish
Scorpion fish
John Dory
Halibut
Red mullet
Haddock
Cod
Swordfish
Crawfish
Shrimps
Crayfish
Skate wings
Steak fish, such as tuna, turbot,
    large mackerel

The basic broth
Bones, heads, trimmings from the
    above, including whole fish if small
3–4 shallots or leeks, chopped
3–4 cloves garlic, crushed
2 large tomatoes, skinned, seeded,
    and chopped
3–4 sprigs each of fennel, parsley, and
    thyme
A strip of dried orange peel
About 12 saffron threads
6 white peppercorns, crushed
3–4 large, oval yellow-fleshed
    potatoes, quartered
Salt and ground black pepper

To finish
About ⅔ cups extra virgin olive oil
1 quantity rouille (see p.232)
3–4 day-old bread rolls,
    halved lengthwise
1 clove garlic

1 Scale, trim, and bone the fish as appropriate (or have your fishmonger do this for you), reserving the heads and bones. Cut the larger fish into pieces roughly the same size as the smaller fish.

2 Divide the fish between two plates. The first plate should have firm-fleshed fish such as the blackfish, monkfish, swordfish, and the crustaceans. The second plate should have the soft-fleshed fish, such as sea bass and skate wings.

3 For the broth, put the fish debris, shallots or leeks, garlic, chopped tomatoes, herbs, orange

peel, and saffron in a large soup pot with about 3 quarts of water. Bring to a boil, add salt, and a few peppercorns. Reduce the heat and simmer for 20-30 minutes to extract all the flavor and body. Strain the broth and return it to the pot with the potatoes. Bring all back to a boil.

4 Warm a soup tureen and a large serving dish along with sufficient soup plates for all, and tell everybody you'll be ready in exactly 25 minutes.

5 As soon as the broth and potatoes have come back to a boil, allow 15 minutes for the potatoes to soften. Add the firm-fleshed fish from the first plate, starting with the crustaceans. Sprinkle with the olive oil, cover the pot again, and bring swiftly back to a boil. Boil rapidly for 5 minutes. Lay in the soft fish from the second plate. Bring swiftly back to a boil and continue boiling briskly, uncovered, for another 5 minutes.

6 Take the pot off the heat, remove the fish with a slotted spoon, and transfer it to the serving dish.

7 Have the rouille ready in a warm bowl. Toast the bread, rub the crumb with a cut clove of garlic, spread with a little rouille, and place the slices in the warm tureen. Dilute the remainder of the rouille with a ladleful of hot broth. Ladle a little of the broth over the bread in the tureen and wait until it goes spongy, 1-2 minutes. Ladle in the rest of the broth.

8 Set the tureen, fish platter, and rouille bowl on the table at the same time. Provide a warm soup plate and a fork and spoon for each guest, along with a large napkin, finger bowls, and a communal plate for the little bones. Hand out more bread, untoasted, to accompany. Everyone eats as he or she pleases, helping themselves from the tureen, fish platter, and the rouille. The Marseillais usually eat the soup first, then the fish and potatoes, but you may do as you please.

Shrimp & Coconut Soup
with Rice Noodles

Serves 4–6

8 ounces rice vermicelli
4 tablespoons oil (sesame or soy)
4 ounces beansprouts, trimmed of any
  brown bits
1 teaspoon finely chopped lemon grass
2 tablespoons dried shrimp paste or
  fish sauce, or 2 salted anchovies
2 small onions or shallots,
  finely chopped
1 teaspoon ground turmeric
2½ cups coconut milk
8 ounces shrimps, shelled
Salt

To finish
4–6 small mint sprigs
1 lime, quartered
Fresh red or green chile, seeded and
  sliced

1 Soak the rice vermicelli in a bowl of very hot water for 10 minutes to swell, then drain and toss with 1 tablespoon of the oil. Divide the noodles among four soup bowls, top with the beansprouts and set aside.

2 Drop the remainder of the oil into a food processor or blender. Add the lemon grass, shrimp paste, fish sauce, or anchovies with the shallots and turmeric and process to a paste.

3 Fry the mixture gently in a large saucepan until the mixture smells fragrant, stirring to prevent burning. Add the coconut milk, bubble up, and add the shrimps. Bubble up again for just long enough for the shrimps to turn opaque. Taste and add salt.

4 Ladle the soup over the vermicelli and the beansprouts and finish each portion with a mint leaf. Serve with the quartered lime for squeezing and chopped chile for those who like it hot.

Portuguese Fisherman's Stew

Serves 6

6½ pounds mixed soup fish, including blackfish, dogfish; also possible are skate, monkfish, red mullet, and sea bass

2¼ pounds shellfish, such as cockles, mussels, clams, razor shells (optional)

⅔ cup olive oil

3 glasses white wine (about 1½ cups)

1 tablespoon white wine vinegar

1 tablespoon mild pimentón (Spanish paprika)

1 tablespoon salt

2¼ pounds potatoes, peeled and thickly sliced

2¼ pounds ripe tomatoes, sliced

3–4 large onions, thinly sliced

3–4 cloves garlic, crushed with salt

1 bay leaf, crumbled

1 Prepare the fish as necessary (bone, scale, clean and so on) and cut into thick steaks.

2 Rinse the shellfish, if using, then allow to soak for 3–4 hours until they spit out their sand.

3 Have ready a roomy, deep-sided, flameproof casserole. In a bowl, mix the oil with the wine, vinegar, pimento, and salt until well blended. If using shellfish, start with these, otherwise begin with the potatoes, layering the fish with the vegetables, garlic, and bay leaf to create as many layers as is convenient for the shape of the casserole. Pour over the oily dressing and leave to stand for 1–2 hours.

4 Carefully bring to a boil and cover as soon as steam begins to rise. Allow to simmer gently for an hour or so, or until all is tender—or transfer to the oven and bake at 320°F. Check occasionally and add boiling water, if necessary.

5 Allow the stew to cool a little before serving. When serving, push a spoon through all the layers so that each person gets a fragrant slice of everything.

• Good with with Salsa Piri-piri (see p.236) or whatever chili sauce you please.

Greek Fish Soup

with Egg & Lemon

Serves 4–6

About 4½ pounds white fish, scaled
  and gutted but left whole
4 tablespoons olive oil
2–3 ribs celery (green, unblanched),
  chopped
1 large onion, thinly sliced
2 tomatoes, skinned and chopped
1 pound large new potatoes,
  quartered lengthwise
Salt and ground black pepper

To finish
2 egg yolks
Juice 1 large lemon
1–2 lemons, quartered

1 Salt the fish thoroughly and set it aside. Bring just under 1 quart water to a boil in a large saucepan with the oil, celery, onion, tomatoes, and potatoes. Cover loosely and simmer for about 15 minutes, or until the potatoes are nearly soft.

2 Rinse the salt off the fish and lay it carefully on top of the potatoes. Bring the broth back to a boil, reduce the heat, and cover the pan. Cook for another 8-12 minutes, or until the potatoes are perfectly tender and the fish is done—you will have to judge this for yourself by parting the flesh down the backbone with a knife: the bone should no longer be pink.

3 Carefully lift out the fish and vegetables with a slotted spoon and divide among 4-6 warm soup bowls. Taste the broth and add salt if necessary.

4 Whisk the egg yolks with the lemon juice in a bowl. Whisk in a ladleful of the hot broth. Remove the pan from the heat and whisk in the frothy egg mixture. Ladle the broth over the fish in the bowls. Serve with the lemon quarters.

Fish Soup with Paprika

Serves 4–6

About 6½ pounds river fish (carp,
   whitefish, pike) or any white fleshed
   sea fish (cod, haddock)
2¼ pounds onions, finely chopped
1 teaspoon dill or fennel seeds
2 heaping tablespoons mild paprika
2 ounces egg noodles
Salt

To finish
1 tablespoon chopped fresh dill
1 level tablespoon chili powder
⅔ cup sour cream

1 Rinse the small fish and gut but don't scale
them. Behead and gut the larger fish and cut
them into thick cutlets.

2 Put the small fish and the heads of the larger
ones into a large saucepan. Add 4½ cups of
water, bring to a boil, reduce the heat, and simmer
uncovered for 1 hour, or until the fish is mushy.

3 Push the broth through a strainer or potato
ricer, making sure all the little threads of flesh
drop through, but leaving the bones behind.

4 Return the broth to the pan and add the
onions, dill or fennel seeds, and the paprika.
Stir, bring to a boil, reduce the heat, and cover
loosely. Simmer gently for 30 minutes, or until the
onions are perfectly tender. Taste and bring up the
flavor with salt (freshwater fish has no natural salt).
Add the noodles, and bubble up and cook until soft.

5 Add the larger fish cutlets and poach them
gently in the fish broth until firm and opaque
—they will need only 3-4 minutes. Divide the broth
and fish among 4-6 warmed bowls and garnish
with chopped dill. Mix a ladleful of the hot broth
with the chili powder and hand it round separately.
Serve with sour cream and plenty of country bread
for mopping.

Catalan Fish Soup

Serves 4 as a main dish

1 pound live mussels
1 pound monkfish tail, filleted
1 pound sea bream, filleted
12 ounces squid, cleaned
2–3 tablespoons all-purpose flour
⅓ cup olive oil
1 small onion, thinly sliced
2 cloves garlic, finely slivered
1 pound ripe tomatoes, skinned,
     seeded, and diced
1 short cinnamon stick
About 12 saffron threads, toasted in a
     dry pan
1 small glass dry sherry or white wine
12 large raw shrimps or langoustines
2 tablespoons chopped fresh parsley
Salt and ground black pepper

1 Scrape the mussels and remove their beards. Put them in a roomy saucepan with 1 quart of lightly salted water.

2 Bring to a boil, cover, and cook for 5 minutes or so, until the shells open. Remove the pan from the heat and transfer the mussels with a slotted spoon to a warm serving dish. Discard any mussels that remain closed.

3 Strain the broth through a cloth-lined strainer—mussels are hard to rid of all their sand. Set aside.

4 Chop the fish fillets into bite-sized pieces and slice the squid into rings, leaving the tentacles in a bunch. Dust the fish through a plateful of seasoned flour.

5 Heat the oil in a roomy skillet. Fry the floured fish for 2–3 minutes on each side, until firm and golden. Transfer to the serving dish with the mussels. Reheat the pan and gently fry the onion and garlic until it softens—don't let it brown.

6 Add the tomatoes, cinnamon, and saffron and bubble up until the tomato collapses, mashing it down to make a thick sauce. Add the sherry or wine and bubble up to evaporate the alcohol.

7 Add the mussel broth and bubble up stirring to blend. Taste and season with pepper.

8 Lay the shrimps in the hot broth, bubble up, and cook briefly until they turn opaque. Transfer the shrimps to the serving dish.

9 Bubble up the sauce again until thick and rich. Ladle the sauce over the fish and finish with a generous sprinkling of parsley.

Fish Soup with Saffron

Serves 4–6

1 knifetip of saffron (about 20 threads)
1¼ quarts fish stock (see p.16)
1 large onion, diced
1 carrot, diced
1–2 bay leaves
½ teaspoon crushed peppercorns
2 cups live mussels or clams, soaked,
    scrubbed, and (if using mussels)
    bearded
8 ounces white fish fillets (swordfish,
    bass, mullet, hake)
8 ounces shrimp
Sea salt

To finish
1 teaspoon grated lemon zest
1 tablespoon chopped fresh parsley

1 Toast the saffron in a dry pan until the scent rises, about 2-3 minutes.

2 In a large saucepan, bring the fish stock to a boil with the onion, carrot, bay leaves, and peppercorns. Crush the saffron into a spoonful of boiling water—use the back of a spoon—and stir it into the stock.

3 Reheat the stock to just boiling, and add the mussels or clams. Return the broth to a boil and cover to allow the shells to open in the steam, discarding any that do not open.

4 Remove the lid, add the fish fillets, and poach them for 2-3 minutes, or until the flesh is firm and opaque.

5 Add the shrimp to the pan. Return the mixture to a boil and remove from the heat. Taste and adjust the seasoning.

6 Ladle into warm soup plates and finish with a sprinkle of lemon zest and chopped parsley.

Mussel Soup

Serves 4-6

2 quarts mussels
1 cup dry white wine
1 bay leaf
3 tablespoons extra virgin olive oil
1 large onion, chopped
2 cloves garlic, finely chopped
4 ounces long-grain white rice
1 pound tomatoes, skinned and
  chopped, or canned plum tomatoes
A strip of orange zest (finger-length)
1 tablespoon chopped fresh parsley
1 tablespoon chopped fresh basil
1 teaspoon chopped fresh cilantro
1 cup unsweetened coconut milk
Salt and ground black pepper

To serve
2 tablespoons olive oil and
  1 teaspoon paprika
Piri-piri or chili sauce

1 Scrub the mussels and scrape off the beards when you are ready to cook them. Bring the wine to a boil with the bay leaf in a large saucepan. Add the mussels, return the pan to a boil, and cover. Cook over a high heat for long enough to open the mussels, 5-6 minutes.

2 Remove the mussels, discarding any that remain closed. Strain and reserve the liquor.

3 Heat the oil in a heavy pan over a medium heat and sauté the onion and garlic until translucent. Add the rice and turn it in the hot oil. Add the tomatoes and let it all bubble up for a couple of minutes.

4 Add the orange zest, mussel liquor, and 1¼ quarts of boiling water to the pan. Bring to a boil and cover. Simmer for 10 minutes, stirring from time to time.

5 Stir in the parsley, basil, and cilantro and season with salt and pepper. Simmer for another 5 minutes, then stir in the coconut milk. Bring back to a boil, add the mussels, and continue cooking until the rice is tender—a few minutes more.

6 Serve the soup in deep plates and finish with a trickle of olive oil blended with a little paprika (dende—palm oil—is traditional). Hand round piri-piri or chili sauce separately.

Scottish Tweed Kettle

Serves 4–6

4–6 salmon steaks (about 4 ounces
  each)
1½ pounds potatoes, sliced
1 large onion, thinly sliced
2 tablespoons chopped chives
Salt and freshly ground black pepper

For the butter sauce
1¾ sticks (14 tablespoons) butter
1 tablespoon vinegar
2 hard-boiled eggs, freshly chopped

1 Wipe over the salmon steaks, salt them lightly,
and set them aside.

2 Place half the potatoes in the bottom of a heavy
saucepan, cover with the sliced onion, and top
with the rest of the potatoes. Pour in enough boiling
water to cover the potatoes completely—about
2 quarts—and add 1 teaspoon salt.

3 Bring the pan to a boil, cover tightly, and
simmer for about 30 minutes. Alternatively, you
can use a casserole and cook the potato mixture in
the oven preheated to 350°F. You may need to add
a little more boiling water. Five minutes before the
end of the cooking time, lay the salmon steaks on
top of the potatoes and season with generous
amounts of pepper.

4 Return the broth to a boil and cover. The fish
will take no longer than 5 minutes to cook
through. Finish with chopped chives.

5 To make the butter sauce, melt the butter in a
small pan, whisk in the vinegar, and stir in the
chopped hard-boiled eggs.

6 Ladle the potatoes, onion, and salmon steaks
into warm serving bowls and hand round the
butter sauce separately.

POULTRY & GAME SOUPS

- Chicken Velouté
- Colombian Hearty Chicken Soup
- Chicken Soup with Saffron & Rice
- Chicken Ghivetch with Rice Noodles
- Chinese Hot-and-Sour Chicken Broth
- Mexican Chicken Soup with Chilaquiles
- Scottish Cock-a-Leekie
- Goose & White Bean Soup
- Polish Chicken Soup with Kreplach
- Turkish Chicken & Yogurt Soup with Walnuts
- Normandy Pheasant Soup with Chestnuts & Cream
- Indonesian Chicken & Coconut Soup
- Spanish Chicken Soup with Chickpeas
- Rabbit Soup with Beer
- Thai Hot-and-Sour Duck Soup

CHAPTER FOUR

POULTRY & GAME SOUPS

Chicken Velouté

Serves 4–6

1¼ quarts chicken stock (see p.15)
2–3 tarragon stalks
1 chicken breast fillet, skinned
  and sliced
About 6 tablespoons heavy cream
3 egg yolks
1 ounce unsalted butter
1 ounce all-purpose flour
¼ teaspoon freshly grated nutmeg
Salt and freshly ground black pepper

To finish
½ cup sour cream
2 tablespoons tarragon leaves

1 Heat the chicken stock in a saucepan until boiling, add the tarragon stalks and bubble the stock rapidly until its volume is reduced by a third, about 15–20 minutes. Slip in the chicken, reheat until boiling, and poach for 5–6 minutes, or until firm and cooked right through.

2 Remove the chicken with a slotted spoon and reserve. Remove the tarragon stalks and reserve the broth.

3 Shred the chicken and drop it into a food processor or blender. Add a ladleful of the broth and process thoroughly until you have a smooth paste. Add the cream and the egg yolks, and process until smooth.

4 Gently melt the butter in a large saucepan, stir in the flour and fry until golden—don't let it brown. Gradually whisk the reserved broth into the pan, making sure there are no lumps. Bring the broth to a boil and bubble up until it thickens and no longer tastes of raw flour, about 5–10 minutes. Remove the pan from the heat.

5 Tip the contents of the food processor or blender into the soup and whisk until well blended. Reheat gently, still whisking, until the soup is just below boiling point. Taste and season with nutmeg, salt, and pepper.

6 Ladle into soup bowls and finish each portion with a spoonful of sour cream and a few tarragon leaves, to garnish.

Colombian Hearty
Chicken Soup

Serves 4–6

2 quarts chicken stock (see p.15)
1 pound cassava, peeled and diced
1 pound yellow-fleshed potatoes,
    peeled and diced
8 ounces chicken breast fillet, diced
1 plantain or unripe banana,
    skinned and diced
2 tablespoons corn kernels
Salt

For the salsa
2 ounces fresh cilantro
6 scallions, diced
1 teaspoon ground cumin
4 tablespoons lemon or lime juice
2 fresh chiles, seeded and diced

To finish
Quartered lemons or limes
Fresh tortillas

1 Bring the stock to a boil in a large saucepan with the cassava and potatoes. Skim off any foam that rises, reduce the heat, and cover loosely. Simmer for 20–30 minutes, or until the potatoes and cassava are tender.

2 Add the diced chicken and plantain or banana. Return to a boil, reduce the heat, and cook for another 10 minutes, or until the chicken is firm. Stir in the corn, reheat until boiling, then remove the pan from the heat. Taste and add salt.

3 To make the salsa, transfer a ladleful of the hot broth to a food processor or blender and add all the salsa ingredients. Process until you have a fragrant, peppery green sauce. Either stir this into the soup or hand it round separately. Serve with lemon or lime quarters and warm tortillas. (To warm the tortillas, wrap them in foil and heat gently in a low oven.)

Chicken Soup

with Saffron & Rice

Serves 4-6

1 pound chicken joints
2 large carrots, scraped and diced
1 pound turnips, peeled and diced
2 large leeks, finely sliced
3–4 ribs celery, chopped
1 small onion, quartered
2–3 cloves
$\frac{1}{2}$ teaspoon white peppercorns
Bouquet garni: small bunch bay leaf,
   rosemary, marjoram, thyme
Salt

The filling
About 3 ounces round-grain rice
$\frac{1}{2}$ teaspoon saffron soaked in
   1 tablespoon boiling water
2 ripe tomatoes, skinned, seeded,
   and diced

1 Put the chicken in a large saucepan with the vegetables, spices, and herbs. Season with salt. Add water to cover—you will need at least 2½ quarts. Bring the water to a boil, cover the pan, and turn down to a simmer. Let cook gently (no large bubbles should break the surface) for 30–40 minutes, until the chicken meat is dropping off the bones and the broth is well-flavored.

2 Strain the broth through a strainer placed over a bowl. Discard the vegetables, pick the chicken meat off the bones, and reserve.

3 Return the broth to the pan, and bring it back to a boil. Stir in the rice. Add the saffron and its soaking water (for added potency, drop the saffron and its water in the blender and process briefly). Return to a boil, lower the heat, and simmer for 20–30 minutes, until the rice is perfectly tender and the broth has turned a sunny gold.

4 Taste and season. Stir in the diced tomato and the reserved chicken meat. Reheat the soup and ladle it into bowls—white, for preference, the better to admire the color—making sure everyone gets their share of rice and chicken.

• Good with Garlic Bread (see p.243).

Chicken Ghivetch

with Rice Noodles

Serves 4–6

4 tablespoons olive oil
1 small onion, diced
3–4 cloves garlic, chopped
2 ounces rice-shaped noodles
1 pound plum tomatoes, skinned,
   seeded, and diced (or use canned)
1¼ quarts chicken stock (see p.15)
1–2 bay leaves
1 short cinnamon stick
1 tablespoon small soup noodles
Salt and freshly ground black pepper

To finish
About 2 ounces feta cheese, crumbled
1 tablespoon mint leaves

1 Heat the oil in a medium saucepan and fry the onion and garlic until softened and golden. Stir in the rice-shaped noodles and cook until the grains turn transparent, about 2–3 minutes.

2 Add the tomatoes and stir over the heat until they go mushy, about 2–3 minutes. Add the stock, bay leaf, and cinnamon. Bring to a boil, reduce the heat, and cover loosely. Cook gently for 20–30 minutes, or until the rice-shaped noodles are tender.

3 Stir in the soup noodles and cook for another 5–10 minutes. Taste and adjust the seasoning.

4 Ladle into soup bowls and finish with crumbled feta cheese and a few mint leaves.

Chinese Hot-and-Sour

Chicken Broth

Serves 4

2 quarts chicken stock (see p.15)

2–3 dried chiles

1 tablespoon soy sauce

3–4 dried tree ear mushrooms

1 can bamboo shoots, drained and slivered

4 ounces fresh firm tofu, diced

1 egg, forked to blend

2 tablespoons rice wine vinegar (or white wine vinegar)

1–2 scallions, finely chopped

Salt and freshly ground black pepper

1 In a large saucepan, bring the chicken stock to a boil and bubble it up until reduced to 1¼ quarts of well-flavored broth. Strain through a strainer lined with a clean cloth. Return the broth to the pan with the chiles and soy sauce. Reheat until boiling and remove from the heat. Leave to infuse for 10 minutes, then remove and discard the chiles.

2 Meanwhile, set the mushrooms to soak in boiling water until they soften and double their size; remove the hard stalks and tear the caps into small pieces.

3 Add the mushrooms to the soup, return it to the heat, and bring back to a boil. Reduce the heat and simmer for 10 minutes. Add the bamboo shoots and diced tofu, and reheat until boiling. Make a whirlpool in the middle and pour in the egg in a steady stream through the tines of a fork, keeping the pan on a boil so that the egg sets in delicate spidery strands. Stir in the vinegar, taste, and adjust the seasoning. Place a little chopped onion into each soup bowl and ladle the broth over.

Mexican Chicken Soup

with Chilaquiles

Serves 4–6

1¼ quarts chicken stock (see p.15)
1 chicken breast fillet, skinned
Oil for shallow frying
8 day-old cornmeal tortillas, sliced
   into fine strips

For the extras (choose from)
2–3 large ripe tomatoes, skinned,
   seeded, and diced
1 mild onion or 3–4 scallions,
   finely chopped
1–2 avocados, pitted, skinned,
   and diced
Few cilantro or epazote sprigs or mint
   leaves, roughly chopped
Quartered limes, for squeezing
Puffy pork cracklings (chicharrónes)
Grated cheddar-type cheese
   (queso añejo)
Pickled chiles (chipotles or moras)

1 Bring the stock to a boil in a large saucepan. Add the chicken breast and simmer for about 10 minutes, or until the meat is perfectly firm. Remove with a slotted spoon and shred thinly.

2 Meanwhile heat a finger's width of oil in a skillet and fry the tortilla strips, a few at a time, until puffed and crisp. Transfer to a paper towel to drain.

3 Provide everyone with a bowl and a spoon, and set the extras out on the table, along with the shredded chicken and the crisp tortilla strips (chilaquiles). Return the broth to a boil while everyone fills their bowls with whatever accompaniments they fancy.

4 Ladle the broth into the bowls, warning everyone not to burn their tongues at the first sip. Some people like a squeeze of lime juice and a nibble of pickled chile. If you have managed to find freshly prepared chicharrónes, add them after you've eaten some of the broth as they will soak up the broth like little sponges and become wonderfully soft and glutinous.

Scottish Cock-a-Leekie

Serves 4–6

4 pounds chicken wings and
    drumsticks
4 pounds leeks, weighed with their
    green tops
1 teaspoon sea salt
1/2 teaspoon peppercorns (white
    for preference)
1 short cinnamon stick
2 cloves
4–6 prunes (soaked or unsoaked)
Salt and freshly ground black pepper
Chopped fresh parsley, to garnish

1 Rinse the chicken pieces and pack them in a large saucepan with 4 quarts of water. Bring to a boil and skim off the gray foam that rises. Meanwhile, trim the leeks, saving the outer leaf trimmings and tops. Slice the remainder thinly, keeping the white and green parts in separate piles.

2 Add the leek trimmings and tops to the broth, return it to a boil, then add the sea salt, peppercorns, cinnamon, and cloves. Turn the heat to low, cover loosely and leave to bubble gently for 1 hour, or until the broth is well flavored and the meat is dropping off the bones.

3 Remove the pan from the heat and tip everything into a strainer set over a bowl to catch the broth. Pick out the chicken meat and reserve, discarding the bones, skin, and other debris.

4 Return the broth to the pan and bring back to a boil. Add the white part of the leeks to the broth. Add the prunes. Return the pan to a boil, reduce the heat, cover loosely and bubble gently for 30 minutes, or until the leeks are soft and almost melted into the broth—mash them a little to help them along. By now the broth should have reduced by a third, concentrating the flavor. If not, bubble it up until the volume is right. If it has lost too much volume, add some boiling water.

5 Cut the remaining leek greens into matchsticks, working with the grain, and stir them into the broth. Return the reserved chicken to the broth.

6 Reheat until boiling and cook for 2–3 minutes, just long enough to soften the leeks without losing their brightness. Check the seasoning and ladle into hot soup plates, finishing each plateful with a generous sprinkling of parsley.

• Good with Oatcakes (see p.246) and fresh cream cheese—crowdie—speckled with chopped chives, just as they like it in the Scottish Highlands.

Goose & White Bean Soup

Serves 4–6

1 piece goose or duck confit
   (leg or wing)
1 pound cooked white or navy beans
   (canned is fine)
1¼ quarts chicken or beef stock
   (see pp.15 & 17)
2 cloves garlic, chopped
2 tablespoons tomato paste
Salt and freshly ground black pepper

To finish
1 teaspoon dried thyme
1 teaspoon dried marjoram
4–5 tablespoons stale bread, cubed
Butter or oil, if necessary

1 In a skillet, gently heat the goose or duck confit until the fat runs. Save the fat. Separate the meat with its skin from the bones. Shred the meat and skin and reserve.

2 Put the bones in a saucepan with the cooked beans. Add the stock, garlic, and the tomato paste and bring to a boil. Skim off any gray foam that rises, turn the heat down to a simmer and cook gently for about 30 minutes, or until the beans are mushy.

3 Drop half the beans and a ladleful of the cooking broth in a food processor or blender and process to a puree, adding more broth if the beans clog up the blades. Stir the puree back into the soup. Taste and adjust the seasoning. Dilute with a little boiling water if necessary—the soup should be thick enough to hold the croûtons.

4 Meanwhile, melt the reserved goosefat in a small skillet and fry the shredded goose meat briefly until the skin crisps and the meat browns. Remove and reserve. Add the herbs and bread cubes to the pan (you may need a little butter or oil) and stir them over the heat until they absorb the fat and the fragrance of the herbs. Continue to stir until they are crisp.

5 Reheat the bean soup and ladle into warm bowls. Serve with crisp goose meat and herby croûtons.

Polish Chicken Soup

with Kreplach

Serves 4–6

2½ quarts chicken stock (see p.15)
2–3 ribs celery, diced
1 large carrot, peeled and chunked
1 onion, chopped
½ teaspoon black peppercorns

For the kreplach dough
1½ cups all-purpose flour
½ teaspoon salt
1 large egg
Chopped parsley, to garnish

For the filling
1 tablespoon chicken fat or oil
1 small onion, finely chopped
1 cup finely chopped cooked chicken
   or minced raw chicken
1 tablespoon finely chopped
   fresh parsley
1 egg, forked to blend
Salt and freshly ground black pepper

1 In a large saucepan, bring the stock to a boil with the celery, carrot, onion, and peppercorns, and boil uncovered until reduced by half, about 30 minutes. Strain the broth through a cloth-lined strainer and return it to the pan.

2 Meanwhile make the kreplach. In a large bowl, work the dough ingredients together until perfectly smooth and elastic (you may need more flour or a dash of water). Shape it into a ball, put it into a plastic bag and leave it to rest while you prepare the filling.

3 For the filling, heat the fat or oil in a small pan and fry the onion gently until it turns transparent. Add the chicken and fry gently if raw; if cooked, just mix in. Add the remaining filling ingredients and mix well together. Season with salt and pepper.

4 Roll out the kreplach dough as thinly as you can (as for ravioli) and cut into squares about the size of your palm.

continued …

5 Drop a teaspoonful of the filling into the middle of each square, brush the edges with a little water and fold over the corners diagonally to make a triangle, pinching the edges to seal. Bring the long points together and pinch firmly to make a ring (the same shape as tortellini). Leave to rest for 15–20 minutes.

6 Bring the chicken broth back to a boil and slip in the kreplach a few at a time, making sure you keep the broth on the boil so that the kreplachs don't stick to the bottom of the pan. Continue in this way for about 20 minutes, until the kreplachs come to the surface. Ladle into bowls and finish with a generous sprinkle of chopped parsley.

Tip
Kreplach is traditionally served at Purim, Rosh Hashannah on the day before Yom Kippur. The noodle dough is rich and soft and not too difficult to make.

Turkish Chicken
& Yogurt Soup with Walnuts

Serves 4–6

2 boned chicken thighs, skinned
   and sliced
1¼ quarts chicken stock (see p.15)
2 ounces walnut pieces
1½ quarts plain yogurt
1 egg yolk
Salt

To finish
1 small onion, finely sliced into half-
   moons
2 tablespoons butter
1 teaspoon dried mint (or 2 teaspoons
   finely chopped fresh mint)

1 Put the chicken and stock in a medium saucepan and bring to a boil. Cover loosely and reduce the heat to a gentle simmer. Leave to cook for 30–40 minutes, or until the chicken is tender and the stock has reduced to 1½ quarts of well-flavored broth. Allow to cool to finger temperature.

2 Meanwhile grind the walnuts to a powder in a food processor or blender. Add the broth and chicken to the processor and process until well blended. Add the yogurt and the egg yolk, and process again. Return the soup to the pan and reheat very gently, whisking throughout, until just below boiling point. Simmer for 5 minutes, or until the soup has thickened a little. Taste and add salt.

3 Meanwhile, prepare the finishing ingredients: fry the onion in the butter until brown and beginning to blacken, then add the dried or fresh mint and remove from the heat.

4 Ladle the soup into bowls and finish each portion with the buttery, mint-flavored onions.

• Good with toasted Pita Bread (see p.242).

Normandy Pheasant
Soup with Chestnuts & Cream

Serves 4-6

1 mature pheasant, cleaned and jointed
2 ounces unsalted butter
1 large onion, diced
1 cup dry champagne or white wine
1 bay leaf
Sprig of thyme
$\frac{1}{2}$ teaspoon ground allspice
1 pound peeled chestnuts
1 cup thick heavy cream
Salt and freshly ground black pepper

To finish (optional)
4 ounces wild mushrooms (ceps,
　chanterelles, pieds-de-mouton)
2 ounces unsalted butter

1 Wipe over the pheasant joints and remove any stray feathers.

2 Melt the butter in a saucepan and add the onion. Stir over the heat for 1-2 minutes and add the pheasant joints. Fry gently for 10 minutes or so, until the meat seizes and takes a little color.

3 Add the wine and 2 quarts water and bring to a boil. Turn down the heat, add the bay leaf, thyme, allspice, season with salt and pepper, cover loosely, and simmer for 30-40 minutes, until the meat is tender. Strain the broth and pick out the bones, reserving the meat.

4 Return the broth to the pan, add the chestnuts, reheat until boiling (add more water if necessary) and simmer for another 30 minutes, until the chestnuts are soft and floury. Mash a little to thicken the broth.

5 Meanwhile, shred the pheasant meat (or dice it finely) and return it to the soup. Stir in the cream, bubble up again and ladle the soup into bowls. Finish with the optional mushrooms, cleaned, sliced, and lightly sautéed in the butter.

• Good with Cheese Straws (see p.239) or Croûtons fried crisp in butter (see p.224).

Indonesian Chicken

& Coconut Soup

Serves 4–6

12 ounces chicken breast fillet, skinned
2 tablespoons vegetable oil
1 medium onion, slivered vertically
2 cloves garlic, crushed
1 teaspoon ground coriander
1 teaspoon chili powder
1 teaspoon ground ginger
1 teaspoon ground turmeric
1 lime leaf or bay leaf
$^1/_2$ lemon grass stalk or 1 strip of lemon zest
2 tablespoons lime or lemon juice
2 cups coconut milk
2 ounces cellophane noodles, soaked for 10 minutes to swell
Salt

To finish
Leaves from a few mint sprigs
$^1/_2$ cucumber, peeled and cut into matchsticks

1 Cut the chicken into thin slivers, salt lightly and set aside.

2 Heat the oil in a medium saucepan and fry the onion and garlic until they soften—don't let them brown. Stir in the spices, lime or bay leaf, and lemon grass or lemon zest. Add the lime or lemon juice and 1 tablespoon of water. Bubble up, reduce the heat and simmer for 10 minutes.

3 Remove the lemon grass or lemon zest and discard. Add the chicken and simmer for another 5 minutes, or until firm and opaque. Add the coconut milk and 1 cup of water and bubble up again. Stir in the noodles and bring back to a boil. Taste and add more salt if necessary.

4 Ladle into bowls and finish with mint leaves and cucumber.

Spanish Chicken Soup
with Chickpeas

Serves 4–6

1 pound chickpeas, soaked overnight
   in water
$^1/_2$ head of garlic
Short length ham bone or
   bacon knuckle
2 chicken quarters (a boiling fowl is
   best; a chicken will do)
6–8 black peppercorns
$^1/_2$ teaspoon coriander seeds
1 onion, roughly chopped
1 bay leaf and a sprig of marjoram
Salt

To finish
1–2 large potatoes, cut into bite-
   sized pieces
Generous handful of spinach or chard
   leaves, shredded
2 tablespoons olive oil

1 Drain the chickpeas and put them in a saucepan with water to cover. Bring to a boil and skim off the gray foam that rises.

2 Hold the clump of garlic in a flame until the papery covering blackens at the edges and the air is filled with the fine scent of roasting garlic cloves. Drop it into the pan with the ham bone and chicken quarters. Add the peppercorns, coriander seeds, onion, and bay leaf and marjoram. Do not add salt. Bring to a boil and reduce the heat. Cover and cook for 1½–3 hours, or until the chickpeas are quite soft.

3 Keep the soup at a gentle bubble—don't let the temperature drop or add salt as this will toughen the skins of the chickpeas and they will never seem to soften. If you need to add water, make sure it is boiling. Add the potatoes 30 minutes before the end of cooking and stir in the spinach 10 minutes before the end. Just before you are ready to serve, add salt and stir in the olive oil.

Rabbit Soup with Beer

Serves 4–6

1 pound rabbit meat, diced
2 tablespoons butter or oil
1 tablespoon diced bacon
1 large onion, diced
1 large carrot, diced
1 celeriac root, diced
1 teaspoon juniper berries, crushed
2 ounces prunes, soaked for 4 hours
    to swell
2 cups lager (Belgian gueuze, for
    preference)
Salt and freshly ground black pepper

To finish
Chopped scallion

1 Fry the rabbit meat in the butter or oil, in a medium saucepan until it stiffens and browns a little. Remove and reserve. Add the bacon, onion, and carrot and fry gently until they take a little color.

2 Return the rabbit to the pan and add the diced celeriac, juniper berries, prunes, and beer. Bubble up until the steam no longer smells of alcohol. Add 1¼ quarts of water and return to a boil. Reduce the heat, and cook gently, loosely covered, for 1 hour. Add more boiling water if necessary. Mash the vegetables a little to thicken the broth. Taste and adjust the seasoning.

3 Ladle into soup bowls and garnish with chopped scallion. Serve with thickly sliced rye bread, crisp red radishes, and unsalted butter.

Thai Hot-and-Sour

Duck Soup

Serves 4–6

12 ounces duck breast (magret),
   slivered
1¼ quarts chicken stock (see p.15)
3 lemon grass stalks, diced, or 3 strips
   of lemon or lime zest
2–3 shallots, diced
2 teaspoons grated fresh turmeric or
   1 teaspoon ground turmeric
1 teaspoon grated fresh ginger
1–2 kaffir lime leaves
2 tablespoons chopped scallions
2 tablespoons chopped cilantro leaves
Sea salt

For the *nam prik*
1 medium eggplant
6 bird's eye chiles (fresh or dried),
   seeded and diced
3 cloves garlic, roughly crushed
1 tablespoon brown sugar
1 tablespoon Thai fish sauce, or
   anchovy sauce, or 2 salt-cured
   anchovies
2 tablespoons lemon or lime juice

1 Lightly salt the slivers of duck breast and set aside.

2 Bring the chicken stock to a boil in a medium saucepan with the tender inner part of the lemon grass or the lemon or lime zest. Add the shallots, turmeric, ginger, and kaffir lime leaves. Reduce the heat and simmer gently for 10 minutes, to marry the flavors. Slip in the duck breast, return the broth to a boil and bubble up for 2-3 minutes, or until the meat is firm.

3 Meanwhile make the *nam prik*. Hull and roughly chop the eggplant. Put all the ingredients in a food processor or blender and process everything to a pulp. (This is ready to use immediately—tangy and delicious, with a real chili kick—but if you need to keep it, store it in a screwtop jar under a thin film of oil, in the refrigerator for no longer than a week).

4 Stir the scallions and cilantro into the broth and ladle into bowls. Hand round the *nam prik* separately for people to add their own.

• Good with Sizzling Rice Crisps (see p.249).

MEAT SOUPS

- French Pot au Feu
- Steak Soup
- Austrian Beef Broth with Bacon & Butter Dumplings
- Trinidad Pepperpot Soup
- Greek Lamb Soup with Cinnamon & Quince
- Hungarian Lamb Soup with Paprika & Cream
- Scotch Broth with Lamb & Barley
- Pork & Vegetable Soup with Pinch-Finger Dumplings
- Irish Bacon & Cabbage Soup
- Beef & Pumpkin Soup with Noodles
- Sweet-and-Sour Pork & Cabbage Soup
- Austrian Ham Broth with Pancake Noodles
- Andalusian Oxtail Soup
- Japanese Shabu Shabu
- Jambalaya with Spare Ribs & Okra
- Beef & Carrot Soup with Parsnip Ribbons

CHAPTER FIVE

MEAT SOUPS

French Pot au Feu

Serves 4-6

2 pounds beef rib, rolled and tied

2 pounds beef foreshank, chunked and tied

1 knucklebone or marrow bone, chunked

2 medium onions, unskinned and quartered

1 small celery head, chopped

½ teaspoon black peppercorns

1–2 bay leaves

2–3 large carrots, chunked (save the trimmings)

2–3 large leeks, chunked (save the trimmings)

3–4 large potatoes, chunked

1 small firm, green cabbage (Savoy)

To finish

Aïoli—garlic mayonnaise (see p.231)

Radishes, capers, cornichons

1 Put all the beef into a large saucepan. Cover with 4 quarts of cold water. Bring to a boil and skim off the foam. Add the onions, celery, peppercorns, bay leaves, and leek and carrot trimmings. Return the pan to a boil, allow one big belch, then reduce the heat. Cover loosely and simmer for 2-3 hours, until the broth is well flavored and reduced by a third.

2 Strain the broth, discarding the trimmings and vegetables and reserving the meat. Remove the fat from the broth: either leave it to cool overnight, then lift off the solid layer of fat or carefully skim off the fat with a spoon while the broth is still hot.

3 Reheat the broth and add the carrots and leeks. Bubble up, reduce the heat, and cook for 10 minutes. Add the potatoes and bubble up again. Reduce the heat and cook for another 10 minutes. Core the cabbage and slice it through the heart, creating a fan shape with the leaves joined at the base. Add to the pan. Bubble up again and cook for 10 minutes more, or until all the vegetables are tender. Check the seasoning.

4 Slice the meat so that everyone gets a share and reheat it with a ladleful of hot broth. Ladle the remainder of the broth and vegetables into warm soup plates and place the meat on top.

5 Hand round a garlicky aïoli, along with side dishes of radishes, capers, and cornichons. There must also be plenty of bread for mopping and large napkins to catch the drips. You'll also need a carafe of rough red wine to enable your guests to *faire chabrot*, a gesture of appreciation made by pouring the wine into the last ladleful of hot soup and drinking it directly from the bowl.

Steak Soup

Serves 4–6

¾ stick (6 tablespoons) butter
3 tablespoons all-purpose flour
2 quarts beef stock (see p.17)
1 large onion, diced
1 large carrot, diced
1 cup corn kernels
1 cup red wine
2 tablespoons red wine vinegar
2 tablespoons tomato paste
1 tablespoon Worcestershire sauce
1 pound minced steak (use lean
    beef mince)
Salt and freshly ground black pepper

To finish
2 tablespoons chopped parsley

1 Melt all but 1 tablespoon of the butter in a large saucepan and stir in the flour. Fry gently for 2–3 minutes, or until it turns golden and takes a little color—don't let it burn. Slowly add the beef stock, stirring or whisking continuously until smooth, then bubble up until it no longer smells of raw flour, about 10 minutes.

2 Add the vegetables, wine, vinegar, and tomato paste, with the Worcestershire sauce and seasonings. Return to a boil, reduce the heat, and simmer for 30 minutes, or until the vegetables are soft.

3 Meanwhile fry the minced steak in the remaining butter until brown, turning it with a spatula to avoid large lumps. Stir the meat into the soup and simmer for another 15 minutes to marry the flavors.

4 Ladle into warm bowls and garnish with plenty of chopped parsley before serving.

Austrian Beef Broth

with Bacon & Butter Dumplings

Serves 6–8

For the broth

2 pounds foreshank of beef (tied in a piece)

2 pounds smoked bacon (tied in a piece)

2–3 mature carrots, chopped

1 Hamburg parsley or a small parsnip, diced

Small bunch of parsley, chopped

½ celeriac or 4 ribs celery, chopped

2 onions

2–3 cloves garlic

1 teaspoon ground allspice

½ teaspoon black peppercorns

For the dumplings

½ stick (4 tablespoons) unsalted butter

1 egg, lightly forked to blend

3 ounces all-purpose flour

Salt

To finish

Chopped fresh parsley and chives

1 Put all the broth ingredients in a large saucepan and pour in enough water to cover generously —about 2 quarts. Bring to a boil, skim off any gray foam that rises and reduce the heat. Cover loosely and simmer gently for 2 hours, or until the meats are tender. Add more boiling water if necessary. (The water should just tremble, no more.)

2 Meanwhile, make the dumplings. In a warm bowl, beat the butter until creamy. Beat in the egg and then fold in the flour and a little salt. Beat well until you have a smooth paste. Cover and let rest for 30 minutes.

3 Remove the meats when they are quite soft and reserve. Strain out and discard the flavoring vegetables (for a good, clear broth, strain the stock through a strainer lined with a clean cloth). Boil the remaining broth until it reduces to about 2 quarts.

4 Using a teaspoon and a clean wet finger, drop little blobs of the dumpling paste into the boiling broth. Turn down the heat to a gentle simmer and poach the dumplings for about 15 minutes, or until firm and light. Ladle the broth and dumplings into hot bowls. Finish with slices of the reserved meat and a good sprinkle of chopped parsley and chives.

Trinidad Pepperpot Soup

Serves 4–6

1 pound stewing beef, cubed
8 ounces diced pork belly, including
   the skin
2–3 chicken joints, chopped into
   bite-sized pieces
2 large onions, thickly sliced
1 Scotch-bonnet chile, seeded
   and chopped
1 short cinnamon stick
3–4 cloves
1 level teaspoon allspice
   berries, crushed
About 1 tablespoon vinegar
About 2 tablespoons dark brown sugar
1 pound sweet potato, diced
8 ounces callaloo greens or
   spinach, shredded
Salt

To finish
Pickled chiles
Quartered limes

1 Put all the ingredients except the sweet potato and greens into a flameproof casserole. Add enough water to cover everything generously—at least 1¼ quarts. Bring to a boil, reduce the heat and cover tightly. Simmer for 1½–2 hours. Alternatively, transfer the casserole to the oven and cook at 300°F.

2 Add the diced sweet potato and cook for 1–1½ hours until the meat is perfectly tender and the cooking juices well reduced. Or you can cook the sweet potato separately and add it at the end of cooking.

3 Dilute the pepperpot juices with enough boiling water to return the soup to its original volume. Reheat and stir in the shredded greens, bubble up for 5 minutes, or until the leaves soften and collapse. Taste and adjust the seasoning with a little more sugar or a touch more vinegar, if needed.

4 Ladle into bowls and serve with pickled chiles and quartered limes.

Greek Lamb Soup
with Cinnamon & Quince

Serves 4–6

1 pound stewing lamb, trimmed and
  diced
2 tablespoons butter
1 pound pickling onions, skinned
  and quartered
$\frac{1}{2}$ cup prunes, pitted or not, as
  you please
1 cup cooked chickpeas, drained
3–4 cloves (stick them into an onion
  quarter for ease of retrieval)
1 short cinnamon stick
2 quarts beef, chicken, or vegetable
  stock (see pp.17, 15, & 14) or water
Juice of 1 lemon
1 ripe quince or 2 yellow-fleshed
  apples, peeled and diced
Salt and freshly ground black pepper

To finish (optional)
2 tablespoons toasted flaked almonds
2 tablespoons pomegranate seeds

1 Rinse the meat and pat it dry. Heat the oil or butter in a medium saucepan and fry the onions gently, shaking the pan over the heat until they take color. Push the onions to one side and fry the meat until it firms and browns a little, about 5 minutes.

2 Add the prunes, chickpeas, and spices with the stock or water. Bubble up, reduce the heat, and cover loosely. Let simmer gently for 1 hour, or until the meat is tender and the broth is well flavored.

3 Taste and season with salt and pepper. Add enough lemon juice to sharpen the flavor. Fold in the diced quince or apple. Bring back to a boil and simmer until the fruit is soft, about 5–10 minutes (don't let it collapse completely). You may need to add a little boiling water to keep the volume.

4 Ladle the soup into bowls and finish, if you like, with a sprinkle of toasted almonds and a few pomegranate seeds.

Hungarian Lamb Soup

with Paprika & Cream

Serves 4–6

1 pound stewing lamb, finely diced
2 medium onions, thinly sliced
2 large carrots, diced
1 celeriac root, diced
Hamburg parsley or small bunch flat
    leaf parsley, finely chopped
1 teaspoon allspice berries, crushed
2 heaped tablespoons mild paprika
1 teaspoon hot paprika or chili powder
Salt and freshly ground black pepper

To finish
½ cup sour cream
1 tablespoon chopped fresh marjoram

1 Put all the ingredients in a medium saucepan with 1¼ quarts of cold water. Bring to a boil and reduce the heat. Cover and simmer gently until everything is tender and the soup is well flavored, about 30 minutes. Add more boiling water as necessary to maintain the volume while the soup is cooking.

2 Ladle into soup bowls and finish each portion with a spoonful of sour cream and a pinch of chopped marjoram.

Scotch Broth

with Lamb & Barley

Serves 4–6

2 pounds pearl barley, soaked for
  3–4 hours to swell
4 ounces neck of lamb, chunked
1–2 bay leaves
2 pounds potatoes, diced
2 large carrots, diced
2 good-sized leeks, sliced (save the best
  of the trimmings)
1 large yellow turnip, diced
Salt and cracked peppercorns

To finish
Chopped fresh parsley

1 Strain the barley, reserving the soaking water. Make up the volume of water to 2½ quarts. Put the meat into a roomy flameproof casserole with the barley and the water. Season with salt and cracked peppercorns. Add the bay leaves, bring to a boil, and reduce the heat. Cover and leave to simmer gently for 1 hour, or until the meat is dropping off the bone. After the first 30 minutes, add the vegetables and more boiling water, if needed.

2 When the meat is soft enough to eat with a spoon and the vegetables have almost collapsed into the broth, it's ready.

3 Ladle into bowls and finish with finely shredded leek trimmings and chopped parsley.

Pork & Vegetable Soup
with Pinch-Finger Dumplings

Serves 4–6

8 ounces stewing pork, diced finely
1 tablespoon vegetable oil or lard
1 onion, slivered
2 cloves garlic, crushed
1 large carrot, diced
1 parsnip, diced
1 pound young turnips (reserve the
    green tops, if any), diced
1 teaspoon caraway seeds
Salt
Chopped fresh dill, to garnish

For the dumplings
1 egg
½ teaspoon salt
About ¾ cup all-purpose flour

1 Put the meat to fry in the oil or lard in a medium saucepan. Let it brown a little, then add the onions and garlic. Let everything fry gently for 10 minutes, then add the carrot, parsnip, and turnips. Fry for another 5 minutes. Sprinkle with caraway seeds, season with salt, and add 2 quarts of water. Bring everything to a boil and reduce the heat. Cover and simmer for 30–40 minutes, or until the meat and vegetables are tender. Taste and add salt.

2 Meanwhile, prepare the dumplings. Fork up the egg with the salt, and work in enough flour to make a soft dough. Knead until it forms a smooth ball, cover with plastic wrap and set it aside.

3 When you are ready to serve, bring a pan of salted water to a boil. Break off small pieces of the dough between your finger and thumb, pressing so that the dough is flattened into a little round cap. Toss the dumplings into the water a few at a time. They are ready as soon they bob to the surface. Transfer them to the soup pan with a slotted spoon. Continue until all are cooked.

4 Finely shred the turnip greens (if available). Reheat the soup and stir in the greens. Bubble up again and cook for 5 minutes, or until the greens are soft. Ladle into bowls and garnish with chopped dill. Serve with pickled cucumbers and black bread.

Irish Bacon &

Cabbage Soup

Serves 4–6

3 pounds bacon knuckle (including the bone and skin), well soaked

½ teaspoon black peppercorns

2–3 cloves

1 bay leaf

1 pound onions, thinly sliced (save the skins for the broth)

1 pound potatoes, sliced

1 pound cabbage, shredded

4 tablespoons chopped fresh parsley

Salt and freshly ground black pepper

Jug of melted butter (allow 1 ounce per person) (optional)

1 Put the bacon in a large saucepan with 2½ quarts of water. Bring to a boil and skim off the foam that rises. Taste the water; if it's very salty, drain it off, then cover with fresh water and proceed as before. Add the peppercorns, cloves, bay leaf, and onion skins (good for color in the broth). Reduce the heat, cover loosely, and simmer for 1–1½ hours, or until the broth is reduced by a third and the meat is perfectly tender.

2 Remove the bacon and carefully lift the meat off the bone. Carve into bite-sized pieces and reserve. Strain the broth and reserve. Layer the onions, potatoes, and cabbage into the pan and cover with the bacon liquor. Bring to a boil and reduce the heat. Cover and simmer for 20–30 minutes, or until the vegetables are soft.

3 Return the meat to the pan and baste it with hot broth. To serve, ladle the soup through the layers, making sure everyone gets their share of all elements. Sprinkle with the chopped parsley and season with salt and pepper. Serve, if you like, with a jug of melted butter. This soup is also good with potatoes cooked in their jackets in a closed pot.

Beef & Pumpkin Soup

with Noodles

Serves 4–6

12 ounces stewing veal or foreshank of
  beef, finely diced

1 large onion, thinly sliced

2 tablespoons butter

1 pound plum tomatoes, skinned,
  seeded, and diced (or use canned)

1 pound pumpkin flesh, diced

1 pound sweet potato, diced

1–2 fresh red chiles (malagueta, for
  preference), seeded and chopped

2 ounces vermicelli

Salt

Salsa piri-piri (see p.236) or other
  chili sauce

1 Put the meat and onion in a roomy flameproof casserole with the butter, and fry gently until the meat and vegetables take a little color. Add the tomatoes and bubble up until the flesh collapses a little, mashing them with a spoon. Add the pumpkin and sweet potato. Bubble up again, reduce the heat, and cover tightly. Cook gently for about 20 minutes.

2 Pour in 2 cups of water—enough to cover the vegetables generously. Reduce the heat, add the chiles, and season with salt. Cover tightly with a lid and simmer gently for 20 minutes, or until the vegetables have softened but not quite collapsed. Add another 2 cups of boiling water and stir in the vermicelli. Cook for another 5 minutes, or until the noodles are perfectly tender. Taste and adjust the seasoning.

3 Ladle into bowls and hand round the salsa piri-piri or other chili sauce separately.

• Good with warm Oatcakes (see p.246) and cream cheese (crowdie) or unsalted butter.

Sweet-and-Sour Pork

& Cabbage Soup

Serves 4–6

8 ounces pork belly (including the
  skin), diced
1 tablespoon oil or lard
2 onions, diced
2 green bell peppers, seeded and diced
1 pound green cabbage, shredded
2 tablespoons chopped fresh dill
2 tablespoons chopped fresh savory
  or tarragon
Salt and freshly ground black pepper

To finish
2 egg yolks
½ cup heavy cream
1 tablespoon wine vinegar
2–3 tablespoons small white grapes,
  halved and seeded

1 In a medium saucepan, fry the diced pork in the oil or lard until the meat begins to brown. Push it aside and add the onions and diced peppers. Season with salt and pepper and fry gently until golden, about 10 minutes. Add the cabbage and herbs, turning to blend. Pour in 2 quarts boiling water. Bubble up and reduce the heat. Cover and cook gently for 20–30 minutes, or until the meat is tender and the cabbage soft. Remove the pan from the heat.

2 Meanwhile, in a small bowl, whisk the egg yolks with the cream and vinegar. Whisk in a ladleful of the hot broth and stir the mixture back into the soup. Gently reheat, stirring, until it thickens a little—don't let it boil.

3 Ladle into bowls and finish each portion with a few halved grapes, peeled or not, as you please.

Austrian Ham Broth

with Pancake Noodles

Serves 4–6

1¼ quarts ham, beef, or chicken stock
   (see pp.18, 17, & 15)
4 tablespoons diced ham
2 tablespoons chopped fresh parsley
½ teaspoon ground allspice
2 heaping tablespoons chopped fresh
   parsley, to garnish

For the pancakes
3 eggs
2 cups all-purpose flour
½ teaspoon salt
1 cup milk
About ½ stick (4 tablespoons) unsalted
   butter

1 Put the stock in a large pan with the ham,
parsley, and allspice. Bring to a boil and simmer
while you make the pancakes.

2 Whisk the eggs with the flour and salt and
slowly add the milk until you have a smooth
lump-free cream. Or drop everything in a food
processor or blender and process to blend.

3 Heat a small skillet—whatever you use to cook
omelets (or pancakes). Drop in a nugget of
butter, wait until it melts and then roll it around the
base of the pan. Pour in a tablespoonful of pancake
batter and tip it around until it forms a thin layer.
When the top surface is dry and the underside is
browned (no more than 2-3 minutes), flip it over
and cook the other side. Transfer to a folded cloth
to keep it soft and warm. Continue until all the
batter is used up.

4 When you are ready to serve, roll the pancakes
up like little carpets and slice them right
through to give narrow ribbons, like tagliatelle.

5 Ladle the boiling broth into warm soup
bowls and divide the pancake ribbons among
the bowls—or hand round separately for people
to add their own. Finish with the parsley. Rye
bread with unsalted butter and radishes are
good accompaniments.

Andalusian Oxtail Soup

Serves 4–6

1 whole oxtail, cut into its sections

2 tablespoons olive oil

4 ounces serrano ham scraps, diced

4 cloves garlic, crushed

1–2 ribs celery, diced

1 carrot, diced

1 pound tomatoes, skinned, seeded,
and chopped (or use canned)

4 ounces white beans, soaked
overnight and drained

1 tablespoon pimentón (Spanish
paprika)

1 short cinnamon stick

3–4 cloves

$\frac{1}{2}$ teaspoon crushed black peppercorns

1 bay leaf

1 cup rough red wine

Salt

Chopped fresh marjoram, to garnish

1 Wipe and trim the excess fat from the oxtail. Heat the oil in a large flameproof casserole or saucepan that will comfortably accommodate all the pieces. Turn the oxtail in the hot oil. Remove, reserve, and replace with the diced ham, garlic, celery, and carrot and fry gently until the vegetables soften. Add the tomatoes and bubble up.

2 Return the oxtail to the casserole with the soaked beans. Add the spices and bay leaf with the wine and bubble up. Add 2 quarts of water—enough to submerge everything generously—and bring back to a boil. Cover tightly and allow to simmer on a very low heat for 3–4 hours, or until the meat is falling off the bones. Alternatively, cook in the oven at 300°F. Check from time to time and add more boiling water to maintain the volume. Taste and add salt.

3 Pick the meat off the bones, and discard the bones. Skim the excess of golden fat from the soup (reserve for other purposes) and return the meat to the pan. Ladle into bowls and finish with chopped marjoram.

• Good today, better tomorrow—particularly with Croûtons fried in the reserved oxtail fat (see p.224).

Japanese Shabu Shabu

Serves 4–6

For the meat and vegetables

1½ pounds tender beef sirloin, slivered

8 ounces dried shiitake mushrooms, soaked in water for 30 minutes to swell, trimmed, and sliced

3 clusters enokitake mushrooms, divided into 3- or 4-stalk bunches

1 cabbage heart, shredded

12 scallions

8 ounces firm tofu, cut into small cubes

For the broth

About 2½ quarts chicken stock or dashi (see pp.15 & 19)

1 small glass sake or other rice wine

2 tablespoons sugar

For the dipping sauce

½ cup tahini

½ cup rice-wine vinegar

½ cup soy sauce

½ cup water

6 tablespoons lemon juice

Accompaniments Plain-cooked sticky rice (1 cup uncooked weight) and pickled cucumbers or vegetables, diced

1 Set out the meat and vegetables on a large serving dish and place this on your dining table.

2 Bring the broth ingredients to a boil in a suitable cooking vessel—in Japan, an earthenware *donabe* (a heat-proof earthenware vessel)—and keep the stock at a rolling boil in the middle of the table throughout the meal. Mix the dipping sauce ingredients together until well blended and provide each person with their own small bowlful. Set out the accompaniments so that each diner can select their own combination.

3 Provide each person with a bowl of sticky rice, a spoon, and chopsticks and allow easy access to the accompaniments as well as the meat and vegetables. You can now serve the soup in one of two ways: tip a batch of meat and vegetables into the boiling soup and allow to cook for 3 minutes, then distribute the cooked food among your guests' bowls with a slotted spoon. Or follow tradition and let each person help themselves with chopsticks, dipping the food into the broth and sauce, holding the bowl beneath to catch the drips.

4 The soup should be ladled into the empty rice bowls and drunk last, when it will be rich with accumulated deliciousness.

Jambalaya

with Spare Ribs & Okra

Serves 4–6

3–4 tablespoons oil

1 pound pork spare ribs, cut into bite-sized chunks

2 tablespoons diced smoked ham

2 ribs celery, chopped

1 large onion, finely chopped

2 cloves garlic, chopped

1 green bell pepper, seeded and chopped

4 ounces okra, trimmed

1 pound skinned, diced tomatoes (or use tinned)

1 cup round-grain rice

$\frac{1}{2}$ teaspoon dried oregano

$\frac{1}{2}$ teaspoon dried sage

1 quart chicken stock (see p.15) or water

Salt and freshly ground black pepper

Louisiana hot sauce or Tabasco sauce, to serve

1 Heat 2 tablespoons of the oil in a flameproof enamel or earthenware casserole and fry the spare ribs, seasoning with salt and pepper as the meat browns. Remove the ribs and set aside.

2 Add the remaining oil and fry the ham, celery, onion, garlic, and green bell pepper gently until soft—don't let anything burn. Add the okra and let if fry for a couple of minutes. Add the tomatoes and bubble up again, mashing them to soften.

3 Return the spare ribs to the casserole and stir in the rice. Add the herbs and the stock or water. Bubble up then reduce the heat. Cover loosely and simmer for about 20 minutes, or until the rice is tender—add more water if necessary. Check the seasoning and ladle into bowls. Hand round a bottle of Louisiana hot sauce or Tabasco separately as appetites for chili vary. Serve with cornbread.

Beef & Carrot Soup
with Parsnip Ribbons

Serves 4–6

4 cups beef stock (see p.17)
2–3 short lengths marrowbone or
   1 pound osso bucco (veal shin)
1 pound large carrots, chopped
1 medium potato, diced
1 medium onion, diced
$\frac{1}{4}$ stick (2 tablespoons) butter
1 tablespoon wine vinegar
$\frac{1}{2}$ teaspoon freshly grated nutmeg
Salt and freshly ground black pepper

To finish
1 parsnip
Oil, for shallow frying

1 In a large saucepan, bring the beef stock to a boil with the marrowbone or osso bucco. Reduce the heat and let simmer for 30-40 minutes, or until reduced by a third. Strain the broth and return it to the pan, reserving the marrow from the bones, if using. (If osso bucco was your choice, shred the meat, toss with a mustardy vinaigrette, and serve with new potatoes.)

2 Bring the broth back to a boil with the carrots and potato. Reduce the heat and simmer for about 20 minutes, or until the vegetables are perfectly tender. Meanwhile, fry the onion gently in the butter in a small pan. Tip the contents of both pans into a food processor or blender and process until smooth.

3 To finish, slice the parsnip into ribbons using a potato peeler. In a small skillet, heat enough oil to submerge the ribbons and fry them, a few at a time, until crisp.

4 Return the soup to the pan, reheat until boiling and stir in the vinegar. Add the nutmeg then taste and adjust the seasoning.

5 Ladle into warm bowls and finish each serving with a little tangle of parsnip ribbons. Scoop the beef marrow, if available, onto crisp little rounds of toast, sprinkle with a few grains of sea salt and chopped fresh parsley and serve it on the side.

VEGETABLE SOUPS

- German Pumpkin Soup
- French Onion Soup
- Curried Parsnip Soup
- Carrot & Fresh Ginger Soup
- Watercress, Leek & Potato Soup
- Herb Soup with Chervil
- Green Pea Soup with Dumplings
- Jerusalem Artichoke Soup with Tapenade
- Sharp-and-Sour Lettuce Soup with Bacon
- Corn Chowder
- Portuguese Cabbage Soup with Olive Oil
- Zucchini & Tomato Soup
- Monastery Mushroom Soup with Sour Cream
- Leek Soup
- Chestnut & Celeriac Soup with Cinnamon
- Cauliflower & Cumin Soup
- Peanut Soup with Greens
- Potato Soup with Pine Nuts
- Red-hot Tomato Soup
- Spinach & Pomegranate Soup
- Minestrone
- Mixed Vegetable Soup
- Spinach & Fennel Bouillabaisse
- Russian Borscht
- Catalan Vegetable Soup-stew

CHAPTER SIX

VEGETABLE
SOUPS

German Pumpkin Soup

Serves 4–6

2 pounds pumpkin flesh, chunked
1 short cinnamon stick
6 cloves
2 tablespoons white wine vinegar
½ stick (4 tablespoons) unsalted butter,
  cut into small pieces
About 1 teaspoon sugar
Salt and freshly ground black pepper

1 Put the pumpkin chunks into a saucepan with the cinnamon and cloves (stick the cloves in a piece of pumpkin for easy retrieval).

2 Add 2 cups of water, bring to a boil, and reduce the heat. Cover the pan loosely and allow to cook gently for 20–30 minutes, or until the pumpkin is perfectly soft. Remove the spices and transfer the pumpkin with its cooking water to a food processor or blender. Process until smooth—add a little more water if necessary.

3 Return the soup to the pan. Stir in the vinegar and reheat until boiling. Stir in the butter and season with salt, plenty of freshly ground black pepper, and a little sugar to bring out the sweetness. Serve with pickled cucumbers and rye bread.

Tip
This is a delicate amber-colored soup flavored with cinnamon, sharpened with vinegar, and enriched with butter. Don't be tempted to add cream or you'll lose its clarity of color and flavor.

French Onion Soup

Serves 4–6

1½ pounds onions, very thinly sliced
   in rings
¾ stick (6 tablespoons) butter
½ cup white wine
3 cups beef stock (see p.17)
Salt and freshly ground black pepper

To finish
4–6 thick slices day-old baguette, cut
   on the slant
About 4 ounces grated cheese

1 In a large saucepan, gently fry the onions in the butter, stirring every now and then, for at least 20 minutes, or until they are soft and golden. Add the wine and stock, season with salt and pepper, bring back to a boil, and reduce the heat. Let simmer for about 20 minutes—longer if more convenient.

2 Meanwhile, preheat the oven to 300°F. Put the baguette slices on a baking sheet in the oven and leave to dry. Divide the slices among the soup bowls, then ladle in the hot soup. The bread slices will rise to the top. Either grate the cheese onto the bread and slip the bowls under the broiler to melt and brown the cheese, or hand round the cheese for people to add their own.

Curried Parsnip Soup

Serves 4–6

2 pounds parsnips, chunked
1¼ quarts vegetable stock (see p.14)
1 tablespoon garam masala

To finish
1 onion, thinly sliced into half moons
¼ stick (2 tablespoons) butter
A few cardamom seeds

1 Put the parsnips and stock in a large saucepan and cook until perfectly tender—allow 20–30 minutes.

2 Drop the parsnips with their cooking liquor into a food processor or blender and process until smooth. Add the garam masala and dilute with a little boiling water if it's too thick or if you have more people to feed. Check the seasoning and reheat until just boiling.

3 Meanwhile, prepare the finishing ingredients. Fry the onion gently in the butter in a small skillet. After 5 minutes, add the crushed cardamom seeds and continue to fry until the onion is golden and perfectly soft, allowing 10–15 minutes.

4 Ladle the soup into warmed soup bowls and finish each serving with a swirl of cardamom-flavored fried onion.

Carrot & Fresh Ginger Soup

Serves 4

2 pounds carrots, sliced
1 potato, diced
1 teaspoon grated fresh root ginger
1 tablespoon cider or white
    wine vinegar
Salt and freshly ground black pepper

To finish
Small handful fresh cilantro,
    roughly torn

1 Put the carrots in a saucepan and add the potato and ginger. Add 1 quart water and cook until the vegetables are perfectly soft. Drop everything into the food processor or blender and process until smooth and thick—dilute with boiling water if necessary. Add the vinegar, taste, and season with salt and pepper.

2 Ladle the soup into warm bowls and finish each portion with a few cilantro leaves.

• Good with Croûtons fried with diced bacon (see p.224).

Watercress, Leek & Potato Soup

Serves 4–6

1 large bunch of watercress
1 large potato, diced
1 large leek, diced
3 cups chicken or vegetable stock
  (see pp.15 & 14)
$\frac{1}{2}$ stick (4 tablespoons) unsalted butter,
  cut into small pieces
$\frac{1}{2}$ teaspoon freshly grated nutmeg
Salt and freshly ground black pepper

To finish
$\frac{1}{2}$ cup sour cream

1 Trim the watercress leaves from the stalks. Reserve the leaves and drop the stalks in a medium saucepan with the potato and leek. Add the stock and bring to a boil. Reduce the heat to a simmer, cover loosely, and cook for 20 minutes, or until the potato is perfectly soft.

2 Transfer the contents of the pan to a food processor or blender and process until smooth. Add the watercress leaves (reserve a few for garnishing) and process briefly again.

3 Return the soup to the pan and reheat until just boiling. Taste and season with salt, pepper, and nutmeg. Swirl in some sour cream and finish with the watercress leaves before serving.

Herb Soup
with Chervil

Serves 4–6

6 ounces chervil
6 ounces other salad herbs (such as
   dandelion, lamb's lettuce, watercress,
   parsley, tarragon, and chicory)
1/2 stick (4 tablespoons) butter
1 large onion, finely chopped
1 large potato, diced
Salt and freshly ground black pepper

1 Pick over and wash the herbs, stripping the leaves from those stalks that are too woody.

2 Melt the butter in a large saucepan and fry the onion gently until transparent. Add the herbs, stir them over the heat for 2–3 minutes, until they collapse. Add the diced potato and 3 cups water. Bring to a boil and then reduce the heat. Simmer for 20 minutes. Mash the potato into the soup to thicken it a little. Taste, and add salt and freshly ground pepper.

• Good with Croûtons (see p.224) fried in butter or bacon fat.

Green Pea Soup

with Dumplings

Serves 4-6

1 pound shelled peas (fresh or frozen)
3–4 scallions or shallots, chopped
½ cup heavy cream
Salt and freshly ground black pepper

To serve
White bread croûtons browned
   in butter (see p.224) or dumplings
   (see p.230)

1 Put the peas and chopped onions in a medium saucepan with 2 cups water. Bring to a boil and reduce the heat. Leave to cook gently for 20-25 minutes, or until the peas are perfectly soft.

2 Push the contents of the pan through a strainer or puree in a food processor or blender. Return the puree to the pan with two-thirds of the cream (reserve the rest). Season with salt and pepper, and bring to a boil, stirring, to blend and avoid sticking.

3 Ladle into bowls and finish each serving with a swirl of the reserved cream. Serve the croûtons or dumplings separately for people to add their own.

Jerusalem Artichoke
Soup with Tapenade

Serves 4–6

1 pound Jerusalem artichokes
About 3 cups vegetable or chicken
    stock (see pp.14 & 15)
1 teaspoon finely grated lemon zest
1 teaspoon ground asafoetida
Salt and freshly ground black pepper

For the tapenade
2 ounces pitted black olives
1 clove garlic, chopped
2 tablespoons extra virgin olive oil
2–3 salt-cured anchovies
1 tablespoon pickled capers, chopped
2 tablespoons lemon juice

1 The knobbly shape of root artichokes makes them tricky to peel unless the skins are loosened first: boil them in a saucepan of salted water for 10 minutes, then rub off the papery covering. Cut the prepared roots into walnut-sized pieces, rinse, and transfer to a medium saucepan with the stock. Bring to a boil, turn down the heat, cover, and let cook until tender, about 25–30 minutes.

2 Drop the artichokes and their cooking water into a food processor or blender and process until smooth. Add the cream and lemon zest and process again. Season with the asafoetida, pepper, and a little salt and return the soup to the pan. Reheat gently, stirring to avoid sticking.

3 Meanwhile make the tapenade. Mash the olives with the garlic, oil, anchovies, capers, and lemon juice, either in the processor or with a pestle and mortar, until you have a smooth paste.

4 Ladle the pale, creamy soup into warm bowls and finish with a swirl of the salty black tapenade—the contrast of color, flavor, and texture is wonderfully dramatic.

• Good with Cheese Straws (see p.239).

Sharp-and-Sour Lettuce Soup with Bacon

Serves 4-6

¼ stick (2 tablespoons) unsalted butter

1 thick slice streaky bacon, diced

2 crisp lettuces (iceberg or cos), rinsed
   and shredded

¼ cup all-purpose flour

½ cup whole milk

2 large eggs

1 tablespoon white wine vinegar

2 tablespoons each chopped fresh dill
   and savory

1 Melt the butter in a medium saucepan, add the bacon, and fry gently until the fat runs and the meat browns a little. Add the shredded lettuces and toss over the heat for 2-3 minutes, or until the leaves wilt. Add 3 cups water and bring to a boil. Turn down the heat and leave to simmer for about 20 minutes.

2 Meanwhile, mix the flour with 2 tablespoons milk until smooth. Whisk in the remainder of the milk, the eggs, and the vinegar. Whisk in a ladleful of the hot lettuce broth, then return everything to the pan and simmer gently until thick and creamy. Ladle into warm bowls and sprinkle with chopped dill and savory. Serve with pumpernickel or rye bread.

Tip
This soup can be served immediately, or let the flavor develop in the refrigerator overnight and serve hot the next day.

Corn Chowder

Serves 4–6

2 cups fresh corn kernels
1 cup light cream or half and half
1 cup milk
Salt and freshly ground black pepper

To finish
1 large ripe tomato, skinned, seeded,
  and diced
1 tablespoon fresh basil leaves,
  shredded
Sliced fresh red chile or chili flakes

To serve
Quartered limes
Tabasco sauce

1 Put the corn kernels in a medium saucepan with 2 cups of water (no salt). Bring to a boil, turn down the heat, and cook for 10 minutes, or until the corn is tender and the cooking liquid has thickened with the starch. Remove 2 tablespoons of the corn with a slotted spoon and reserve.

2 Drop the remainder of the corn and the cooking liquor into a food processor or blender with the cream and milk and process until well blended. Taste, and season lightly with salt and pepper.

3 Return the soup to the pan and reheat gently, stirring continuously, until just boiling. Stir in the reserved corn kernels and diced tomato. Ladle the soup into warm soup bowls and finish with shredded basil leaves and slivers of fresh chile or a few chili flakes.

4 To serve, hand round the limes and Tabasco sauce for people to add what they please.

Portuguese Cabbage
Soup with Olive Oil

Serves 4–6

4–6 medium potatoes (1 per person)
1 onion, finely chopped
1 pound dark green cabbage leaves
(spring greens) or curly kale or
cavalo nero
2 tablespoons extra virgin olive oil
Salt and freshly ground black pepper

To serve
Extra virgin olive oil
Salsa piri-piri (see p.236)

Tip
Only the outer leaves
of a very dark leaved
cabbage will do, and
these must be very
finely shredded.

1 Put 2½ quarts water into a roomy saucepan with the potatoes and onion. Bring to a boil, add salt, and cook for 20 minutes, or until the potatoes are perfectly tender.

2 Meanwhile, shred the cabbage very finely with a sharp knife: first cut out the hard white stalk and central vein of the cabbage leaves, then roll the leaves up in little bundles and shred finely right across the grain.

3 Mash the potato into the broth to thicken, season with pepper, and check for salt, then stir in the oil. Bring the broth back to a boil and sprinkle in the shredded cabbage, stirring continuously, so that it feels the heat immediately. Bubble up fiercely for 3–4 minutes—just long enough to soften the leaves. The cabbage should retain a little bite and the soup remain as green as grass.

4 Ladle into soup bowls. Hand round a jug of extra olive oil and salsa piri-piri for a touch of fieriness from Brazil.

Zucchini & Tomato Soup

Serves 4–6

2 tablespoons olive oil
1 pound onions or shallots, skinned
  and chopped
1–2 ribs celery, thinly sliced
2 pounds tomatoes, skinned and
  roughly chopped
1 cup vegetable or chicken stock
  (see pp.14 & 15)
1 pound zucchini
Salt and freshly ground black pepper

To serve

6 zucchini flowers, shredded, or the
  leaves from 3–4 basil sprigs
Balsamic vinegar
Grated Parmesan cheese

1 Heat the oil in a saucepan and fry the onions and celery gently until they lose their crispness. Add the tomatoes and bubble up, mashing with a fork to collapse the tomato to a thick puree. Add the stock, bring to a boil, cover, and reduce the heat. Simmer for 15-20 minutes, then mash thoroughly or drop everything into a food processor or blender and process until smooth. Gently reheat.

2 Meanwhile, grate the zucchini into a colander, salt them lightly, and leave to drain for 10 minutes or so. Rinse to remove the excess salt.

3 Reheat the tomato and stock and stir in the grated zucchini. Bring back to a boil, reduce the heat, and simmer for another 10 minutes, or until the vegetables are soft and soupy.

4 Ladle into bowls and finish with shredded zucchini flowers or basil leaves and a drop of balsamic vinegar. Hand round a bowl of grated Parmesan separately.

Monastery Mushroom

Soup with Sour Cream

Serves 4–6

8 ounces mixed wild or cultivated
  mushrooms
1/4 stick (2 tablespoons) butter
1 tablespoon diced smoked
  bacon or ham (optional)
2 large leeks, thinly sliced
2–3 ribs celery, thinly sliced
1–2 large carrots, diced
1 bay leaf
1 thyme sprig
1/2 teaspoon freshly grated nutmeg
1 large potato, peeled and grated
Salt and freshly ground black pepper

To finish
1/2 cup sour cream
2 tablespoons chopped fresh chives
  (or chopped leek green)

1 Pick over the mushrooms, wipe the caps, trim the stalks, and slice. Melt the butter in a medium saucepan and stir in the mushrooms. Fry for a moment before adding the bacon or ham, if using. The wetter the fungi, the longer it takes to release their water and caramelize a little.

2 As soon as the mushrooms have yielded up their water and started to sizzle, add the leeks, celery and carrots and fry for another 5 minutes, or until the vegetables soften. Add the herbs and 1 1/4 cups water and bring everything to a boil. Season with freshly grated nutmeg, salt, and pepper, and reduce the heat. Cover loosely and let simmer for about 40 minutes.

3 Stir in the grated potato and bring back to a boil. Simmer for another 10 minutes, or until the potato is perfectly soft and has thickened the broth.

4 Check the seasoning and ladle into bowls. Finish with a swirl of sour cream and a sprinkle of chopped chives. Serve with thick slabs of brown bread and Gouda or Edam cheese, plain and wholesome.

Leek Soup

Serves 4–6

6 large leeks, with their green
1 large potato, diced
$\frac{1}{3}$ cup olive oil
4 cloves garlic, halved vertically
Ground allspice or freshly grated
    nutmeg, to taste (optional)
2–3 tablespoons chopped fresh parsley
Salt and freshly ground black pepper

1 Bring $1\frac{1}{4}$ quarts of water to a boil in a saucepan, and salt lightly. Meanwhile, trim the leeks: discard the root and remove the tough outer leaves but leave most of the green. Cut the leeks lengthwise into long, thin ribbons. Stir the leeks into the boiling water, bubble up, and reduce the heat. Leave to simmer for 10 minutes, or until the leeks soften. Add the potato and bubble up again. Reduce the heat and cook gently for another 15–20 minutes, or until the potato is perfectly soft.

2 Meanwhile, warm the oil in a small skillet and fry the garlic gently until small bubbles form around the edges and they start to brown. Remove the pan from the heat, take out the garlic, and discard, reserving the oil.

3 Mash the potato into the broth just enough to thicken it a little. Stir in the garlicky oil and bubble up. Reduce the heat and then raise it again so that the oil and the broth form an emulsion. Taste and season with salt and pepper and a little ground allspice or grated nutmeg, if liked. Stir in the parsley. Serve with toasted bread rubbed with garlic and oil.

Chestnut & Celeriac

Soup with Cinnamon

Serves 4–6

12 ounces fresh unskinned chestnuts
1 pound celeriac, diced
3 cups vegetable or chicken stock
  (see pp.14 & 15)
1 short cinnamon stick
2 egg yolks, forked to blend
$\frac{1}{2}$ stick (4 tablespoons) butter,
  chopped into small pieces
Salt and freshly ground black pepper
1–2 teaspoons ground cinnamon,
  to garnish

1 Prick the chestnuts in one or two places with a fork or the point of a knife and drop them into a saucepan with enough cold water to cover. Bring to a boil and cook the chestnuts in their jackets for about 15 minutes. Drain and transfer to a bowl of cold water to loosen the skins. Remove both the tough outer shell and the russet inner skin.

2 Put the peeled chestnuts back into the pan with the diced celeriac, the chicken or vegetable stock, and the cinnamon stick. Bring to a boil, reduce the heat and simmer for 30–40 minutes, or until the chestnuts are perfectly soft.

3 Remove the cinnamon stick and reserve a few of the whole chestnuts.

4 Push everything else through a strainer or transfer to a food processor or blender and process until smooth.

5 Return the soup to the pan, taste, and add salt and freshly ground pepper. Whisk in the egg yolks and the butter. Reheat carefully without allowing the soup to reboil.

6 Serve the soup in bowls, finishing each portion with the reserved whole chestnuts and a sprinkle of the ground cinnamon.

Cauliflower &

Cumin Soup

Serves 4–6

1 small cauliflower, trimmed and
  separated into florets
1/2 stick (4 tablespoons) unsalted butter
2 medium onions, diced
1 teaspoon ground cumin
2 cups whole milk
Salt and freshly ground black pepper

To finish
2–3 tablespoons diced tomato
1/2 teaspoon cumin seeds
2–3 cilantro sprigs

1 Cook the cauliflower florets for 15-20 minutes, in just enough lightly salted water to cover, until they become soft. Drain, reserving 1 cup of the cooking water.

2 Meanwhile, melt the butter in a medium saucepan and gently fry the onions until they soften—don't let them brown. Sprinkle with the cumin and remove from the heat.

3 The contents of the pan into a food processor or blender with the cauliflower and the reserved cooking water. Add the milk and process thoroughly until smooth.

4 Reheat until boiling and ladle into bowls. Finish each portion with a teaspoon of diced tomato, a sprinkle of cumin seeds, and cilantro leaves.

Peanut Soup

with Greens

Serves 4–6

12 ounces spinach or any other
  edible greens
1 pound tomatoes, skinned, seeded,
  and chopped
6–8 scallions, finely chopped
4 ounces unsalted, shelled, roasted
  peanuts
Salt
1 teaspoon chili flakes, to garnish

1 Cook the spinach in a tightly lidded saucepan in the water that clings to the leaves after washing, sprinkling with $\frac{1}{2}$ teaspoon salt to encourage the juices to run.

2 As soon as the leaves collapse and soften, remove the lid and add $1\frac{1}{4}$ quarts of water, tomatoes, and chopped scallions. Turn down the heat, cover loosely, and simmer for about 15 minutes, or until the tomato flesh has collapsed in the steam.

3 Meanwhile, crush all but a tablespoon of the peanuts in a food processor or blender

4 Stir the crushed peanuts into the soup, cover loosely, and simmer for another 15 minutes.

5 Taste and adjust the seasoning, ladle into bowls, and finish with the reserved peanuts and a sprinkle of chili flakes.

Potato Soup
with Pine Nuts

Serves 4–6

2 pounds potatoes, thickly sliced
3¾ quarts beef stock (see p.17) or
   water
1 large clove garlic, chopped
1 large onion, finely chopped
Salt and freshly ground black pepper

To finish
4 tablespoons pine nuts
1 tablespoon chopped fresh chives

1 Put the potatoes in a large saucepan with the stock or water. Add the garlic and onion and bring to a boil. Reduce the heat, cover loosely, and cook for about 30 minutes, or until the potato has more or less collapsed into the broth. Mash roughly so that the soup stays fairly lumpy—don't process.

2 Meanwhile, lightly toast the pine nuts in a dry pan. Set aside 1 tablespoon for finishing and crush the rest roughly. Stir the crushed pine nuts into the soup and simmer for another 10 minutes.

3 Taste and adjust the seasoning. Ladle into bowls and finish with the reserved pine nuts and chopped chives. Serve with soft white rolls.

Red-hot Tomato Soup

Serves 4–6

2–3 tablespoons extra virgin olive oil
1 onion, finely chopped
2–3 cloves garlic, crushed
2–3 peperoncini or any fresh or
 dried chiles
2 pounds tomatoes (fresh or canned),
 roughly chopped
1 thyme sprig
1 oregano sprig
Sugar, salt, and ground black pepper

To finish
2 tablespoons chopped fresh parsley
1 tablespoon black olives, pitted
 and chopped

1 Put all the ingredients except the seasonings into a large saucepan and leave to infuse for 30 minutes. Bring everything to a boil, then reduce the heat. Simmer gently over a low heat for 30 minutes. You shouldn't need to pay it much attention as the tomatoes produce plenty of liquid and there is little danger of sticking.

2 Push the tomato mixture through a fine-meshed strainer, leaving skin, seeds, and other debris behind.

3 Return the puree to the pan and dilute with water to the consistency that suits you (2 cups is a rough guide). Bring back to a boil and season with sugar, salt, and freshly ground black pepper.

4 Ladle into bowls and finish with a sprinkling of chopped parsley and chopped pitted black olives.

Spinach

& Pomegranate Soup

Serves 4–6

1 pound spinach, stalks removed, rinsed
1/4 stick (2 tablespoons) butter
1 large onion, finely chopped
1 tablespoon ground turmeric
2 tablespoons long grain rice
2 tablespoons yellow split peas
1/2 teaspoon crushed black peppercorns
1 teaspoon salt
Juice and finely grated zest of 1 bitter orange or lemon
The seeds of 1 pomegranate

1 Shred the spinach and set it aside.

2 Melt the butter in a large saucepan. Add the onion, turmeric, rice, split peas, peppercorns, and salt with enough fresh spring water to cover generously, about 1¼ quarts. Bring to a boil, reduce the heat, and bubble gently for 20–30 minutes, or until the rice grains are tender and the split peas are perfectly soft. Stir in the spinach and bubble up again. Reduce the heat, and simmer for another 10 minutes, or until the spinach is well amalgamated into the soup. Stir in the citrus juice and zest, then taste and adjust the seasoning.

3 Ladle into bowls and finish each portion with a sprinkle of pomegranate seeds.

• Good with one of the Middle Eastern flatbreads such as Pita Bread (see p.242).

Minestrone

Serves 4

4 tablespoons olive oil

1 large onion, diced

2 large carrots, diced

2–3 green ribs celery (including the
   leaves), chopped

1 cup ham or vegetable stock
   (see pp.18 & 14)

1 pound old potatoes, diced

1 pound yellow or white turnips,
   peeled and diced

4 tablespoons short macaroni or any
   medium-sized pasta shapes

2 cups shredded cabbage (cavalo
   nero or Savoy)

Salt and freshly ground black pepper

To finish

2 tablespoons finely chopped
   fresh parsley

1 teaspoon finely grated lemon zest

1 clove garlic, finely chopped

To serve

Olive oil, for drizzling

Parmesan cheese, for grating

1 Heat the oil in a large saucepan and fry the onion, carrot, and celery gently for about 10 minutes, or until the vegetables soften and take a little color (sprinkle them with a little salt to help the frying process). Add the stock, the diced potatoes, and turnips, and bring everything to a boil. Allow one big bubble, turn down the heat, cover loosely, and simmer for about 15 minutes, or until the vegetables are nearly soft. Mash the vegetables a little to thicken the broth.

2 Stir in the macaroni or your chosen pasta, reboil, and cook for another 10 minutes. Stir in the shredded cabbage. Bring everything back to a boil and cook for another 5 minutes, or until both the pasta and cabbage are tender. The total cooking time will be about 30 minutes.

3 Just before you serve, stir in the finishing ingredients, taste, and adjust the seasoning. Ladle into warm soup bowls in which you may, if you wish, place a slice of day-old bread (Tuscan bread, which would traditionally be used for minestrone, is unsalted.) Serve with oil for drizzling and a chunk of Parmesan cheese and a grater.

Mixed Vegetable Soup

Serves 4–6

2–3 fresh shallots or young leeks,
 thinly sliced
2–3 young carrots, chopped
1–2 ribs celery with their green,
 chopped
1 green bell pepper, seeded and diced
1 pound small new potatoes, scrubbed
 and halved
2 tablespoons extra virgin olive oil
8 ounces fava beans in their pods,
 diced
8 ounces freshly podded peas
2 tablespoons chopped fresh parsley
1 tablespoon wine vinegar
Salt and freshly ground black pepper

To serve
Almond All-iol-i (see p.231) or Salsa
 Romesco (see p. 236)

1 Put the sliced shallots or leeks, carrots, celery, pepper, and potatoes in a large saucepan with 1¼ quarts water. Add 1 teaspoon salt and a turn of the pepper mill. Bring to a boil and stir in the olive oil. Reduce the heat to a simmer, cover loosely, and let cook for about 20 minutes, or until the potatoes are tender and the oil has blended into the broth.

2 Stir in the fava beans and peas, bubble up again, and cook for another 5 minutes, adding more boiling water if necessary. The consistency should be midway between a stew and a soup. Stir in the chopped parsley and sharpen the broth with a little vinegar. Taste and adjust the seasoning.

3 Serve in deep bowls, handing round an almond al-iol-i or salsa romesco separately for people to stir into their soups. Accompany with plenty of good fresh bread, roughly chunked.

Spinach & Fennel

Bouillabaisse

Serves 4–6

2 pounds spinach, stalks removed,
  shredded
1 large onion, finely chopped
1 fennel bulb, diced
1 pound potatoes (yellow, for preference)
3 cups vegetable stock (see p.14) or
  water and 1 glass white wine
2 cloves garlic, finely chopped
2 tablespoons chopped fresh parsley
About 4 tablespoons olive oil
Salt and freshly ground black pepper

To finish
4–6 poached eggs or shelled soft-boiled
  eggs (optional)

1 Rinse the shredded spinach and set it aside.

2 Put the onion, fennel, and potatoes in a medium saucepan. Add the stock or water and wine. Season lightly. Bring everything to a boil, then reduce the heat. Simmer for 20 minutes, or until the potato is soft.

3 Stir in the spinach, garlic, and parsley and return to a boil. Cook for another 5–8 minutes, or until the spinach has collapsed into the broth.

4 Stir the oil into the broth and bubble up. Reduce the heat until the soup is no longer bubbling, then bubble up again. Repeat at least twice, until you can no longer see traces of oil on the surface and the broth is slightly thickened. Serve in deep soup plates, with or without a poached or soft-boiled egg floated on each portion.

Russian Borscht

Serves 4–6

1 pound uncooked small beets with
their leaves
2 ounces lard or 3 tablespoons oil
1 onion, finely chopped
1 clove garlic, chopped
1 large carrot, diced
1 large parsnip, diced
1 small turnip, diced (include the
leaves, if available)
1¼ quarts chicken or vegetable stock
(see pp.15 & 14)
1 bay leaf
2 medium potatoes, peeled and diced
About 1 teaspoon sugar
1 tablespoon vinegar
Salt and freshly ground black pepper
½ cup sour cream, to serve

1 Rinse the beets and trim the leaves, leaving
a generous tuft of stalk. Drop one of the beets
into a small pan with enough water to cover, bring
to a boil, and cook gently for 20–30 minutes, or
until perfectly tender. Set aside. Meanwhile, peel
and grate the remaining beets, shred the leaves and
chop the stalks.

2 Put the lard or oil in a large saucepan, add
the onion and garlic and fry until they take a
little color. Stir in the grated raw beet, the carrot,
parsnip, and turnip and turn them over in the heat
for 1–2 minutes. Add the stock and bay leaf and
bring to a boil. Reduce the heat and simmer gently
for 10 minutes.

3 Add the diced potatoes. Bring back to a boil
and simmer for 12–15 minutes, or until the
potatoes are soft. Stir in the shredded beet leaves
and diced stalks. Bring back to a boil, season
with salt, pepper, a little sugar, and the vinegar.
Simmer for another 5–10 minutes, or until
everything is soft.

4 Skin and dice the reserved cooked beet, stir it
into the broth, and watch the soup take on a
beautiful crimson blush.

5 Ladle the soup into bowls and hand round a
bowl of sour cream separately. Serve with
black bread and a side dish of radishes and
pickled cucumbers.

Catalan Vegetable Soup-stew

Serves 4–6

4 tablespoons olive oil

1 large Spanish onion, thinly sliced

1 tablespoon diced serrano ham or
lean bacon (optional)

2 red bell peppers, seeded and sliced

1 pound tomatoes, skinned, seeded,
and diced (or use canned)

½ cup white wine

1 pound pumpkin or winter squash,
peeled, seeded, and diced

Salt and freshly ground black pepper

For the picada

2 cloves garlic, chopped

1 tablespoon toasted almonds

2 tablespoons chopped flat leaf parsley

1 teaspoon ground cinnamon

2–3 cloves

½ teaspoon ground cloves

6–8 saffron threads, soaked in
1 tablespoon boiling water

To finish

4–6 thick slices of sourdough bread

1–2 tablespoons olive oil

4–6 tablespoons grated cheese

1 Heat the oil in a saucepan and fry the onion and ham gently for 20 minutes, or until soft and golden. Remove and reserve. Drop in the pepper rings and fry them until they soften. Return the onions to the pan, add the diced tomatoes and the wine, and bubble fiercely until the tomato flesh collapses and the steam no longer smells of alcohol.

2 Add the pumpkin and pour in about 3 cups of boiling water. Return to a boil, reduce the heat, and simmer for 20 minutes, or until the pumpkin is soft. Meanwhile, blend the picada ingredients in a processor or blender, or pound in a pestle and mortar until you have a thick paste—you may need a little more water. Stir the picada into the soup and cook for 5 minutes, to blend the flavors.

3 Meanwhile, toast the bread on both sides, and trickle each slice with a little olive oil. Top the toasts with grated cheese. To serve, ladle the soup into heat proof soup bowls and top each portion with its slice of bread and cheese. Slip the bowls under a hot broiler to melt the cheese.

- Italian Bean &
  Macaroni Soup

- Yorkshire Mushy Pea Soup

- Greek Fava Bean
  & Fennel Soup

- Italian Barley Soup with
  Wild Greens

- Navy Bean Soup with
  Cabbage

- Spanish Green Lentil Soup

- Mexican Black Bean Soup

- Chickpea Soup with
  Cheese & Egg

- Chestnut Soup

- Spicy Chickpea Soup

- Portuguese Red Bean Soup

- Chickpea & Ginger Soup

- Provençal Bean Soup with
  Pistou

- Spiced Green Lentil Soup

- Mung Bean Soup with
  Cashew Nuts

- Caribbean Red Bean Soup

- Borlotti Bean Soup with
  Sour Cream

- Welsh Oatmeal Cawl

- Flageolet & Cornmeal
  Soup with Blue Cheese

- Peruvian Quinoa &
  Pumpkin Soup

- Mulligatawny with Dhal

- Polish Buckwheat
  & Mushroom Soup

CHAPTER SEVEN

PULSE &
GRAIN SOUPS

Italian Bean &
Macaroni Soup

Serves 4–6

4 ounces navy beans, soaked for
  6 hours or overnight
2 quarts ham or vegetable stock
  (see pp.18 & 14)
1 large carrot, diced
2–3 ribs celery, chopped
½ teaspoon crushed black
  peppercorns
2 bay leaves
1 teaspoon dried oregano
1 large tomato, skinned and diced, or
  about 8 ounces diced pumpkin
2 ounces macaroni or any medium-
  sized pasta shapes
1 pound dark green leaves (such as
  cabbage, kale, turnip tops), shredded
Sea salt

To finish
2 tablespoons fresh flat leaf parsley,
  chopped
Extra virgin olive oil

1 Drain the beans and put them in a large saucepan with the stock. Bring to a boil and skim off the gray foam that rises. Add the carrot, celery, peppercorns, bay leaves, and oregano. Bring back to a boil and reduce the heat a little. Bubble gently for 1 hour, or until the broth is well flavored and the beans are soft but not yet mushy.

2 Remove the bay leaves and stir in the diced tomato or pumpkin. Bring back to a boil. Add a little salt, stir in the pasta, and return to a boil. Bubble up for another 15 minutes, or until the pasta is nearly soft. Stir in the shredded leaves, bring back to a boil, and cook for another 5 minutes, or until everything is tender. Check and adjust the seasoning.

3 Ladle into bowls, finish with chopped parsley, and swirl a little olive oil into each serving. Hand round more olive oil for people to add as they please.

Yorkshire Mushy
Pea Soup

Serves 4–6

8 ounces dried marrowfat peas, soaked
   overnight
1¼ quarts bacon or beef stock
   (see pp.18 & 17)
1 cup milk
1 onion, diced
1 carrot, scraped and diced
2–3 ribs celery, diced
1 parsnip, diced
¼ stick (2 tablespoons) butter or lard
Salt and freshly ground black pepper

To finish
2 tablespoons chopped fresh parsley
About ¾ stick (6 tablespoons) chilled
   butter

1 Drain the peas and put them in a saucepan with the stock. Bring to a boil, reduce the heat, and leave to simmer until the peas are mushy —about 40-50 minutes. Stir in the milk.

2 Meanwhile, in a skillet fry the vegetables gently in the butter or lard until they soften. Combine the contents of the two pans, stirring to blend. Taste and adjust the seasoning, then reheat well. Ladle into bowls and finish with a sprinkle of chopped parsley and a pat of butter. Good with slices of a freshly baked farmhouse loaf and a thick slab of crumbly cheddar cheese.

Greek Fava Bean

& Fennel Soup

Serves 4–6

2 pounds shelled fava beans
1 onion, chopped
1 fennel bulb, chopped
1 teaspoon grated lemon zest
Juice of $\frac{1}{2}$ lemon
4 tablespoons olive oil
$1\frac{1}{4}$ quarts water
$\frac{1}{2}$ cup white wine
Salt and freshly ground black pepper

To finish
1 egg whisked with the juice of
  $\frac{1}{2}$ lemon
2 chopped scallions
2 tablespoons chopped fennel fronds
  or dill

To serve
Quartered lemon

1 Pick over the fava beans and slip them out of their skins.

2 Put the beans in a roomy saucepan with the remaining ingredients and bring everything to a boil. Cover and simmer for about 30 minutes, or until the beans are quite tender.

3 Remove the soup from the heat. Whisk a ladleful of the hot broth into the egg and lemon mixture, then whisk it back into the soup. Reheat gently without reboiling or the egg will scramble. Finish with a sprinkle of chopped scallions and fennel fronds or dill.

4 Serve with lemon quarters and plenty of bread to mop up the broth.

Italian Barley Soup
with Wild Greens

Serves 4–6

2 tablespoons olive oil
1 onion, diced
1 carrot, diced
1 celery, diced
1¼ quarts vegetable stock (see p.14)
2 ounces barley, soaked for 2 hours
1 pound new potatoes, scrubbed
   and quartered
1 pound peppery greens (failing wild-
   gatherings, use rocket, sorrel, frizzy
   endive, watercress, chervil, or
   spinach), rinsed and shredded
4–5 scallions or wild garlic (leaves
   only), chopped
Juice and grated zest of 1 lemon
Salt and freshly ground black pepper

To finish
Grated Parmesan cheese

1 In a medium saucepan, heat the oil and fry the onion, carrot, and celery until they soften a little. Add the stock, stir in the barley and its soaking water, and bring everything to a boil. Turn down the heat and let it simmer for 40-45 minutes, or until the barley is tender and has thickened the broth.

2 Add the potatoes—the pieces should be about 1-inch round—and bring back to a boil. Stir in the greens and the scallions or wild garlic. Bring back to a boil and cook for another 5 minutes. Season with salt and pepper.

3 Stir in the lemon zest and enough juice to sharpen the flavor. (The wilder the greens, the less lemon you'll need.)

4 Ladle into soup bowls and hand round the grated Parmesan cheese separately.

Navy Bean Soup

with Cabbage

Serves 4–6

8 ounces navy beans, butter beans, or
  flageolet beans, soaked overnight
1 pound salt pork or unsmoked
  bacon, diced
1 pound tender young turnips,
  chopped
2 pounds old potatoes, peeled and
  chopped
1 small Savoy cabbage or 1 pound
  spring greens, finely shredded
1 tablespoon diced serrano ham
Salt and freshly ground black pepper

1 Drain the beans and put them in a large saucepan with 2½ quarts of water. Bring to a boil, skim off the gray foam that rises and add the pork or bacon. Reduce the heat to a gentle bubble. Cover loosely and leave to cook for 1–1½ hours, or until the beans are perfectly tender, adding more boiling water as necessary, and making sure the level of water remains roughly constant. When the beans are soft, taste and season with salt and pepper.

2 Ladle half the broth into another saucepan, bring to a boil, and add the diced turnips. Return to a boil and add the potatoes. Simmer for 15 minutes, or until the vegetables are nearly soft.

3 Add the shredded leaves and the diced serrano ham. Bring back to a boil, cover, and cook for another 6–10 minutes, or until the cabbage is tender but still green. Stir the contents of one pan into the other and serve the soup in deep soup bowls—or hand the two panfuls separately for people to combine as they please.

• Good with Croûtons fried crisp in bacon fat or fresh pork lard with a little garlic (see p.224).

Spanish Green Lentil Soup

Serves 4-6

8 ounces lentils (the greeny-brown
   ones)
2 tablespoons olive oil
1 onion, chopped
4-5 cloves garlic, unskinned
1 tablespoon diced serrano ham
2 ribs celery, chopped
1 large tomato, skinned and chopped
1 dried red pepper, Ñora, seeded and
   torn or 1 tablespoon pimentón
   (Spanish paprika)
3-4 cloves
$\frac{1}{2}$ teaspoon black peppercorns,
   crushed
1 bay leaf
1 large potato, peeled and diced
Salt

To finish

2 handfuls spinach or chard
   leaves, shredded
2-3 tablespoons olive oil
1 tablespoon each of chopped fresh
   marjoram and parsley

1 Put the lentils in a medium saucepan with 2 quarts of water and bring to a boil.

2 Heat the olive oil in a small skillet and fry the onion, garlic, and ham until they sizzle and begin to brown.

3 Add the contents of the skillet to the soup pan along with the remaining ingredients except the potato. Bring back to a boil and cover loosely. Reduce the heat and leave to simmer for 40 minutes, or until the lentils are beginning to soften. Add the potato and bring everything back to a boil. Season and then turn down to a simmer. Cook for another 15-20 minutes, or until the potatoes and lentils are soft. (Lentils need about 1 hour cooking in all, when they should be quite soft—if they're old, they'll take a longer.) Top up with boiling water if necessary.

4 To finish, stir in the shredded spinach or chard and bubble up for 5 minutes. Stir in the olive oil, taste, and adjust the seasoning. Serve garnished with marjoram or parsley.

• Good with crisp bread Croûtons fried in olive oil with garlic (see p.224).

Mexican Black Bean Soup

Serves 4–6

8 ounces dried black beans, soaked
    for no more than 6 hours or
    two 14-ounce cans ready-cooked
    black beans, drained
1¼ quarts ham stock (see p.18)
Salt

To finish
1 large or 2 small ripe avocados
1 green chile, seeded and diced
Juice of 2 limes
2 tablespoons chopped fresh
    cilantro, plus extra to garnish

1 Drain the beans of their soaking water and put them in a flameproof casserole with the onion and oil or lard. Add 1¼ quarts boiling water—enough to cover the beans generously. Bring to simmering point, then turn down the heat. Cover tightly and leave to cook gently. Alternatively, cook them in the oven preheated to 325°F. Keep an eye on them and add hot water if necessary. Leave them to cook for as long as it takes for the skins to soften completely, about 2 hours (the fresher the beans, the quicker they will cook). Add salt after the beans soften completely.

2 Drop the beans and their liquor into a food processor or blender and process to a puree. Dilute with boiling water to a spooning consistency.

3 If using canned beans, drain and process to a puree with the ham stock.

4 Meanwhile, mash the avocado flesh with the chopped chile, lime juice, and cilantro.

5 Reheat the soup and ladle into soup bowls. Finish each portion with a spoonful of the spicy mashed avocado and an extra sprinkle of cilantro leaves. Serve with quartered limes and chili flakes, and soft tortillas, if liked.

Chickpea Soup

with Cheese & Egg

Serves 4–6

6 ounces chickpeas, soaked overnight
1 large onion, finely chopped
2 carrots, diced
2 ribs celery, chopped
1 teaspoon grated lemon zest
1–2 sprigs each of thyme and rosemary
1–2 bay leaves
4 tablespoons olive oil
Salt and freshly ground black pepper

To finish
2 eggs beaten with the juice of 1 lemon
  and 2 tablespoons of grated cheese

1 Drain the soaked chickpeas. Bring 2 quarts of water to a boil in a large saucepan. Add the chickpeas and the remaining ingredients, except the salt. Bring back to a boil. Cover tightly and leave to cook at a rolling simmer for about 2 hours. Salt the soup when the chickpeas are soft.

2 Whisk a ladleful of the hot broth into the finishing mixture and whisk it back into the soup. Squish the chickpeas down a bit. Do not reboil or the eggs will curdle and your lovely velvety thickening will separate. Serve with bread, handing round more grated cheese separately.

Chestnut Soup

Serves 4–6

6 ounces dried chestnuts, soaked
   overnight
1¼ quarts chicken stock (see p.15) or
   water with ½ cup of white wine
1 tablespoon sugar
½ stick (4 tablespoons) butter
2 egg yolks, forked to blend
Salt and freshly ground black pepper

To finish
1 cup thick strained sheep's milk
   yogurt (or any plain, thick yogurt)
1 tablespoon chopped fresh marjoram

1 Drain the chestnuts and bring them to a boil in a medium saucepan with the stock or water and wine, the sugar, and the butter. Reduce the heat to low, cover tightly, and simmer for 30–40 minutes, or until the chestnuts are soft.

2 Drop everything into a food processor or blender and process until smooth. Add the egg yolks to the mixture and process until well blended.

3 Return the soup to the pan and reheat gently—don't let it boil. Taste, and add salt and freshly ground pepper.

4 Ladle into bowls and finish each portion with a spoonful of yogurt and chopped marjoram.

Tip
Traditionally, this soup is made in the fall with fresh nuts and into the winter with dried ones.

Spicy Chickpea Soup

Serves 4–6

2 pints cooked chickpeas (boiled
   without salt)
Juice of 2 lemons
2 tablespoons coarse salt
2 tablespoons mustard-seed oil
2 teaspoons black mustard seeds
2–3 small dried red chiles, crumbled
   (or fresh chiles, seeded and diced)
1 tablespoon ground asafoetida

To finish
2 tablespoons flaked coconut,
   lightly toasted
2 tablespoons chopped fresh cilantro

1 Put the chickpeas in a food processor or blender with 1¼ quarts of water, the lemon juice, and salt. Process until smooth. Transfer to a saucepan and heat, stirring regularly, until it boils.

2 Heat the oil gently in a skillet, then add the mustard seeds—they jump like fleas when they feel the heat, so have a pan lid handy. Add the chiles and allow to sizzle for a few seconds. Add the asafoetida and immediately stir the panful into the bean soup.

3 Ladle into soup bowls and finish with flakes of toasted coconut and chopped cilantro. Good with chapatis or other flat breads.

Portuguese Red Bean Soup

Serves 4–6, generously

6 ounces red kidney, pinto, or borlotti beans, soaked overnight

4 ounces pork belly skin, cut into thin slivers

1 chouriço negro or morcela, or similar black pudding, or 4 ounces soft chorizo

1 large onion, finely diced

6 cloves garlic, chopped

1 bay leaf

$\frac{1}{2}$ teaspoon white peppercorns

2 small turnips, diced

1 large carrot, diced

1 pound waxy potatoes, peeled and diced

Salt

To finish

Chopped fresh cilantro

A generous handful of salsa piri-piri sauce (see p.236)

1 Drain the beans and put them in a large saucepan with enough cold water to cover generously. Bring to a boil, drain, and return the beans to the pan. Add 2½ quarts of fresh water and bring back to a boil. Skim off any gray foam that rises.

2 Add the pork belly skin, with the sausage, onion, garlic, and bay leaf. Add the peppercorns. Bring to a boil, reduce the heat, and cover loosely. Keep the pan bubbling gently for as long as it takes to tenderize the beans, about 1-2 hours. If you need to add water, make sure it is boiling. Remove the sausage, slice neatly, and keep them warm. Taste and season the broth.

3 Add the turnips, carrot, and potatoes to the pan and bubble up for another 15-20 minutes, or until the vegetables are tender. Add more boiling water if it looks like drying out, remembering that this soup should be very thick and dense with vegetables. Finish with a generous handful of chopped cilantro.

4 Ladle into bowls and hand round salsa piri-piri or some other hot sauce for people to add their own.

Chickpea & Ginger Soup
with Turmeric

Serves 4-6

6 ounces chickpeas, soaked overnight
$2\frac{1}{2}$ quarts unsalted chicken or
   vegetable stock (see pp.15 & 14)
2 ounces red lentils
1 onion, finely chopped
2 tablespoons tomato paste
1 short cinnamon stick
1 tablespoon ground ginger
1 teaspoon ground cumin
1 teaspoon ground turmeric
2–3 dried chiles, seeded and crumbled
Salt and freshly ground black pepper

To finish
3–4 tablespoons olive oil
A handful of fresh cilantro, chopped,
   leaves only
A handful of fresh mint, chopped,
   leaves only
Quartered lemon
Pita bread (see p.242)

1 Drain and rinse the chickpeas, then put them in a large saucepan with the stock. Bring to a boil and simmer for at least 2 hours, or until tender—don't add salt or allow the pan to come off the boil. Add more boiling water as necessary to maintain the volume. When the chickpeas are perfectly soft, stir in the lentils, onion, tomato paste, and spices. Season with salt and pepper. Bring back to a boil and simmer for another 30 minutes, or until the lentils are mushy and the soup is satisfyingly thick.

2 Finish with a swirl of olive oil and a generous handful of chopped cilantro and mint. Serve in deep bowls, with lemon quarters for squeezing and soft pita bread for mopping.

Provençal Bean Soup
with Pistou

Serves 4–6

6 ounces butter beans, soaked
  overnight
2¹/₂ quarts unsalted vegetable stock
  (see p.14) or water
1 bay leaf
¹/₂ teaspoon crushed black
  peppercorns
1 large potato, peeled and diced
Sea salt

For the pistou
4–6 fresh, plump cloves garlic (one for
  each person)
1¹/₄ cups basil leaves, stripped from
  their stems
1 slice day-old bread
¹/₂ cup extra virgin olive oil
Sea salt

To serve
Grated cheese (Cantal or Parmesan)

1 Drain the beans and put them in a saucepan with the stock or water, the bay leaf, and crushed peppercorns—no salt. Bring to a boil, skim off the gray foam that rises, and reduce the heat to a simmer. Cover and let cook gently for 1 hour. Add the potato and continue to cook for a further 30 minutes, or until the beans are soft. Check regularly and add more boiling water as needed.

2 Meanwhile, put all the pistou ingredients in a food processor or blender and process until smooth. Alternatively, pound the garlic, basil leaves, and bread with a pestle in a mortar, then add the oil gradually until you have a thick, spoonable emulsion.

3 When the beans and potatoes are soft, season with salt. Mash or process a ladleful and stir it back into the soup to thicken the broth.

4 Ladle into bowls, finish each serving with a swirl of pistou, and hand round the remainder separately, with a bowl of grated cheese. Provide plenty of fresh baguette for mopping and a bowl of salty black Provençal olives for nibbling.

Spiced Green
Lentil Soup

Serves 6

2 shallots or 4–5 scallions,
  finely chopped
2–3 cloves garlic, finely chopped
3–4 tablespoons oil
8 ounces green lentils
$\frac{1}{2}$ teaspoon ground cumin
$\frac{1}{2}$ teaspoon ground cinnamon
$\frac{1}{2}$ teaspoon crushed dried chiles
1 large potato, diced
Salt and freshly ground black pepper

To finish

2 tablespoons chopped fresh cilantro
2–3 scallions, finely chopped

1 In a roomy saucepan, fry the chopped onions and garlic gently in the oil until soft and golden —don't let them brown.

2 Add the lentils and stir over the heat. Pour in $2\frac{1}{2}$ quarts of water and add the spices. Bring to a boil and season with salt and pepper. Reduce the heat and simmer for 10 minutes.

3 Add the diced potato, bring back to a boil, and cook gently for another 30 minutes, or until the lentils are soupy and the potato is perfectly soft.

4 Taste and adjust the seasoning. Finish with a sprinkle of cilantro and finely chopped scallions.

Mung Bean Soup
with Cashew Nuts

Serves 4–6

4 tablespoons ghee or unsalted butter
4 ounces split mung beans, soaked for
   6 hours
2 ounces long-grain rice
1 teaspoon salt
1 teaspoon cumin seeds
1 teaspoon cracked black pepper
1 tablespoon chopped fresh
   root ginger
$^1/_2$ teaspoon crushed, dried chile

To finish
2 tablespoons toasted cashew nuts,
   roughly chopped, to garnish

1 Heat half the ghee or butter in a medium saucepan. Drain the beans and add to the pan. Fry, stirring for 1–2 minutes. Add the rice and stir briefly over the heat until the grains turn transparent and are coated with fat.

2 Add 2 quarts of water with the salt and bring to a boil. Stir to break up the lumps and reduce the heat. Cover loosely and bubble up for 10 minutes. Stir again, cover tightly, and reduce the heat to a simmer. Allow to cook gently for another 50 minutes, or until the beans are mushy and the rice is tender.

3 Meanwhile, in a small skillet, heat the remaining ghee or butter. Add the spices and allow them to sizzle for a few seconds. Stir the contents of the pan into the soup right at the end of the cooking.

4 Ladle into bowls and garnish with the toasted cashew nuts.

Caribbean Red Bean Soup

Serves 4-6

6 ounces red beans (pinto or borlotti
    or cranberry beans) soaked
    overnight
2-3 shallots, diced
2 ounces long grain rice

For the seasoning mix
2 tablespoons olive oil or butter
2 cloves garlic, finely chopped
1 medium onion, finely chopped
1 red bell pepper, seeded and
    finely chopped
2 tablespoons tomato paste

1 Drain the beans and put them in a saucepan with $2\frac{1}{2}$ quarts of water. Bring to a boil and skim off the gray foam that rises. Stir in the shallots, reduce the heat, and cover loosely. Allow to bubble gently for 1 hour, or until the beans have softened but not yet collapsed.

2 Stir in the rice, adding more boiling water to make up the original volume, and cook for another 20 minutes, or until the rice is tender and the beans are almost mushy. Mash a little to thicken the broth.

3 Meanwhile, prepare the seasoning mix. Heat the oil or butter in a heavy skillet and fry the garlic, onion, and pepper gently until soft—allow 10 minutes—without letting it brown. Add the tomato paste diluted with 2 tablespoons water and bubble up, stirring to blend.

4 Ladle the soup into bowls and finish each portion with a spoonful of seasoning mix.

Borlotti Bean Soup

with Sour Cream

Serves 4-6

6 ounces borlotti beans, soaked
   overnight
1 large potato diced
4 ounces streaky bacon, diced
2–3 tablespoons fresh pork lard
   or butter
2 medium onions, skinned and diced
Salt and freshly ground black pepper

To finish
1 cup sour cream

Tip

You can make the soup with
canned beans in brine: if so, no
need for soaking and preliminary
cooking, drain them and make up
the volume with water (no need
to soak), and cook for just
long enough to soften
the potato.

1 Drain the beans and put them in a saucepan. Cover them generously with fresh water. Bring them to a boil, skim, and reduce the heat. Cook, loosely covered, until perfectly tender—allow 1-2 hours depending on the freshness of the beans. As soon as they are soft, add the potato, bring back to a boil, and season with salt and pepper. Cook until the potato is tender—15-20 minutes—adding more boiling water if necessary.

2 Meanwhile, fry the bacon in its own fat until crisp and brown—you may need a little butter or lard. Remove and reserve.

3 Melt the remaining butter or lard in the pan drippings, add the onions and fry until soft and golden, about 10 minutes. Return the bacon to the pan. Stir the onion, bacon, and the oily drippings into the soup.

4 Ladle into bowls and finish each portion with a spoonful of sour cream.

Welsh Oatmeal Cawl

Serves 4–6

2 quarts bacon or ham stock (see p.18)
2 heaping tablespoons coarse
   ground oatmeal
1 pound potatoes, peeled and diced
8 ounces rutabaga or parsnip, diced
8 ounces carrots, diced
2 large leeks, thinly sliced
Salt

To finish
¹/₂ stick (4 tablespoons) chilled butter
1 tablespoon each chopped fresh
   parsley and chives

1 Put the stock in a saucepan and stir in the oatmeal. Bring to a boil, stirring until smooth. Add the prepared vegetables and bring back to a boil. Reduce the heat to a simmer. Cook gently for about 30 minutes, or until the vegetables are soft and the oatmeal has thickened the broth. Taste and add salt if necessary.

2 Serve in deep soup bowls (wooden bowls and spoons are traditional) and drop a curl of butter into each bowl just before serving. Finish with chopped parsley and chives. Traditional accompaniments are a thick slice of bread and a wedge of crumbly cheese, such as Caerphilly or Cheddar.

Tip
Cawl is a traditional Welsh dish, and is an amalgamation of broth, stew, and soup.

Flageolet & Cornmeal
Soup with Blue Cheese

Serves 4–6

6 ounces flageolet beans, soaked
  overnight or two 14-ounce cans,
  drained
2 quarts ham or vegetable stock
  (see pp.18 & 14)
1 bay leaf
A short length ham bone (optional)
1 tablespoon diced serrano ham
2 tablespoons pork lard or butter
1 tablespoon fine ground cornmeal
Salt and freshly ground black pepper

To finish
4 ounces crumbled blue cheese
  (Cabrales, for preference)

1 Drain the flageolet beans and put them in a medium saucepan with the stock. Bring to a boil and skim off any foam that rises.

2 Add the bay leaf, and the ham bone, if using. Add the diced serrano ham and lard or butter. Bubble up again, reduce the heat, and cover. Allow to bubble gently for 1 hour, or until the beans are perfectly soft (the time it takes depends on the age of the beans). Add boiling water as necessary to maintain the volume.

3 Mix the cornmeal with a little cold water and stir it into the soup. Bring back to a boil and bubble for another 20 minutes, or until the cornmeal has thickened the broth. Taste and season with salt and pepper.

4 Ladle into deep soup plates and finish each portion with crumbled blue cheese.

Peruvian Quinoa
& Pumpkin Soup

Serves 4–6

4 ounces quinoa
1 pound pumpkin or winter squash
flesh, diced
1¼ quarts vegetable or chicken stock
(see pp.14 & 15)
4 tablespoons unsalted butter or
olive oil
Juice and finely grated zest of 1 lime
Salt and freshly ground black pepper

To finish
2 fresh yellow chiles, seeded and
finely chopped
Small bunch of basil, leaves torn

To serve
Quartered limes
Unsalted tortilla chips
(see p.247)

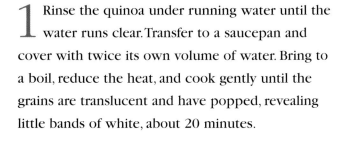

1 Rinse the quinoa under running water until the water runs clear. Transfer to a saucepan and cover with twice its own volume of water. Bring to a boil, reduce the heat, and cook gently until the grains are translucent and have popped, revealing little bands of white, about 20 minutes.

2 Meanwhile put the pumpkin in a pan with the stock, bring to a boil, reduce the heat, and cook until the pumpkin flesh is soft and mushy, about 15-20 minutes.

3 Transfer to a food processor or blender, drop in the butter or oil, and process until smooth.

4 Return the soup to the pan and reheat. Stir in the quinoa, lime juice and zest, then taste and adjust the seasoning.

5 Ladle into bowls and finish with chopped chiles and a few torn basil leaves. Serve with quartered limes and tortilla chips.

Mulligatawny with Dhal

Serves 4–6

4 ounces yellow or orange lentils
2 ounces long-grain rice
2 quarts chicken stock (see p.15)
1 tablespoon curry powder
    (or garam masala)
Salt and freshly ground black pepper

To finish
$\frac{1}{2}$ stick (4 tablespoons) butter
2 onions, thinly sliced
2 cloves garlic, sliced
3–4 cloves
1 short cinnamon stick, broken into
    small pieces

To serve
1 cup plain yogurt stirred with
    chopped fresh mint

1 Pick over and rinse the lentils and put them and the rice in a saucepan with the stock. Bring to a boil. Skim off the gray foam that rises and then stir in the curry powder or garam masala. Reduce the heat and allow to simmer gently for about 1 hour, or until the dhal is perfectly tender and soupy. Season with salt and a generous amount of freshly ground black pepper.

2 Meanwhile, melt the butter in skillet. As soon as it froths, add the onions, garlic, cloves, and cinnamon and fry gently until soft and beginning to brown. Stir the contents of pan into the soup and taste and adjust the seasoning.

3 Reheat and ladle into bowls. Separately, hand round a bowl of yogurt stirred with a handful of chopped mint leaves (chop the mint at the last minute). Poppadums or crisply toasted or fried Bombay duck (a dried fish preparation available in Indian groceries) make a suitable accompaniment.

Polish Buckwheat
& Mushroom Soup

Serves 4–6

8 ounces whole buckwheat

$\frac{1}{2}$ stick (4 tablespoons) butter

$2\frac{1}{2}$ quarts vegetable, ham, or chicken
stock (see pp.14, 18 & 15)

12 ounces mushrooms (wild or
cultivated), sliced

Salt and freshly ground black pepper

To finish

1 cup sour cream

2 tablespoons chopped fresh dill

1 Fry the buckwheat grains in half the butter in a medium saucepan for 2–3 minutes, or until they smell toasty. Add the stock and bring to a boil. Reduce the heat to a gentle simmer, cover tightly, and cook for 40–50 minutes, or until the grains are soft and porridgy (add boiling water if they begin to look dry).

2 Meanwhile, melt the remaining butter in a small skillet, add the mushrooms, and season with salt and pepper. Toss them over the heat until the fungi yield up their water and begin to fry. Stir the contents of the skillet into the soup when the buckwheat is soft.

3 Ladle into bowls and finish each portion with a dollop of sour cream and a sprinkle of chopped dill. Serve with black bread, unsalted butter, and radishes or pickled cucumbers.

SWEET SOUPS

- *Apple Soup with Cinnamon*
- *Hungarian Sour Cherry & Cream Soup*
- *Swedish Rhubarb Soup*
- *Finnish Red Currant & Rye Bread Soup*
- *Three-Berry Soup*
- *Blueberry Soup*
- *Quince Soup with Honey, Wine & Cream*
- *Danish Buttermilk Soup*
- *Apricot Soup with Hazelnuts*
- *Rosemary & Lemon Syllabub*
- *Zabaglione*
- *Chocolate Cream Soup*
- *Mango Water*
- *Saffron Milk*
- *Wine Soup with Cinnamon & Cloves*
- *Portuguese Sopa Dorada*

CHAPTER EIGHT

SWEET SOUPS

Apple Soup

with Cinnamon

Serves 4–6

2 pounds cooking apples, peeled and
  sliced
Finely-grated zest and juice of 1 lemon
2 tablespoons superfine sugar
1 thimble-sized piece of
  cinnamon bark
2–3 cloves
1 cup dry white wine
1 tablespoon cornstarch
1 tablespoon unsalted butter

To finish
3–4 tablespoons fresh white bread
  crumbs
1–2 tablespoons unsalted butter
1 teaspoon ground cinnamon

1 Put the sliced apple, lemon zest and juice in a
medium saucepan. Add the sugar, cinnamon and
cloves (stick them in a piece of apple peel for ease
of retrieval). Add the wine and bring to the boil.
Reduce the heat, cover and leave to simmer for
20-25 minutes, or until the apple collapses into the
cooking liquid.

2 Remove the cinnamon stick and cloves and
mash the apple into the juices, or transfer to a
food processor and process to a puree. Return the
puree to the pan and allow it to cool slightly.

3 Meanwhile, prepare the finishing ingredients in
a skillet: fry the bread crumbs in the butter
until crisp and golden, stirring throughout, and toss
with the cinnamon.

4 Mix the cornstarch with 2 tablespoons cold
water, blending it with the back of a spoon
until smooth. Stir into the soup. (Decide whether
you need to add a little water if the soup looks too
thick or if you need to increase the quantity of
cornstarch). Return the pan to the heat and bring it
back to the boil, beating continuously to avoid
lumps. Turn down the heat and simmer until the
soup thickens a little, about 2-3 minutes. Beat in
the butter.

5 Ladle the soup into small bowls and finish with
a sprinkle of crisp bread crumbs.

Hungarian Sour Cherry

& Cream Soup

Serves 4–6

1 pound sour cherries, pitted
4 ounces sugar
1 heaped tablespoon all-purpose flour
1 cup sour cream, plus extra to serve
   (optional)
$\frac{1}{2}$ teaspoon salt
Brown sugar, to decorate (optional)

Tip

This must be made with fresh fruit—tinned won't do—so if you can't find sour cherries, use sweet cherries and compensate for their sweetness with lemon juice.

1 Put the cherries and sugar in a medium saucepan with 1 quart of water. Bring to a boil and reduce the heat. Cover and cook until the cherries are soft and the juice is a beautiful ruby red, about 15-20 minutes. Rub the fruit and its juice through a strainer, or puree in a food processor (be warned, blenders always bleach out color).

2 Meanwhile, stir the flour into the cream, working to eliminate lumps, and add the salt. Add a ladleful of the cherry puree to the cream and work it thoroughly to blend. Whisk the cream mixture back into the cherry puree (this can all be done in the processor).

3 Return the mixture to the pan and reheat gently until it comes to a boil, whisking throughout. Continue to cook until it thickens a little, about 5 minutes. Cover and allow to cool. Cover the surface with plastic wrap and set the soup in the refrigerator to chill. Finish, if you like, with a dollop of sour cream and a sprinkle of brown sugar. Equally good hot or cold, although the latter is more traditional.

Swedish Rhubarb Soup

Serves 4–6

2 pounds rhubarb, chopped
4 ounces sugar
1 tablespoon cornstarch, arrowroot
  or potato starch

To serve
Cream
Brown sugar
Ground ginger

Tip

The Swedish version of this chilled soup is traditionally served as a dessert. Rhubarb is popular throughout Northern Europe, where it's counted as the first fruit of spring. Good for a picnic—put it in a thermos and serve it out of mugs.

1 Put the rhubarb in a saucepan with the sugar and ⅔ cup water, bring to a boil, cover loosely and simmer until perfectly tender, about 10 minutes. Press the fruit and its juices through a strainer, or drop everything into a food processor or blender, and process until smooth.

2 Meanwhile, in a bowl, blend the cornstarch, with a couple of spoonfuls of water. Add the mixture to the fruit puree and process to blend.

3 Return the soup to the pan, bring back to a boil, stirring until the juice thickens a little. Allow to cool, covering with plastic wrap to avoid the formation of a skin, and chill. It should be really cold when it's served. Hand round the cream, brown sugar and ginger separately.

4 The traditional accompaniment is a bowl of plain rice cooked in milk, but it's delicious with a crisp biscuit.

Finnish Red Currant

& Rye Bread soup

Serves 4-6

1 pound redcurrants, stripped from
  the stalks (use a fork)
3 ounces superfine sugar
4 ounces dry rye bread, crumbled
Lemon juice, to taste (optional)

To serve
Thick sour cream
Brown sugar

Tip
You can make this
soup with any of the
berry fruits—blueberries,
raspberries, blackcurrants,
gooseberries.

1 Bring the redcurrants to the boil in a saucepan with 1½ cups water. Reduce the heat, cover and cook for 10-15 minutes, or until the berries have popped and frothed. Add the sugar, reheat and stir until the crystals have dissolved. Remove from the heat, and press the fruit and its syrup through a strainer to remove the pips. Allow to cool a little.

2 Meanwhile, put the bread to soak in 1½ cups water.

3 Drop the bread and its soaking water into a food processor with the fruit and its syrup, and puree until smooth.

4 Return to the pan, heat to boiling point and simmer for a few moments to thicken the juices, beating throughout. Taste for sweetness or sourness—you might need to add a little lemon juice for sharpness or sugar for extra sweetness.

5 Serve warm, with plenty of thick sour cream and brown sugar.

Three-Berry Soup

Serves 4–6

8 ounces redcurrants, stripped from
  the stalks (use a fork)
8 ounces cherries
8 ounces raspberries
1 tablespoon potato starch or
  cornstarch
2 ounces sugar

To serve
Light cream

1 Put all but a handful of the fruits in a medium
saucepan with 4 cups of water. Bring to a boil,
reduce the heat and simmer for 8-10 minutes, until
the fruit is soft and the juice has turned the
cooking water scarlet.

2 Press everything through a fine strainer or drop
the whole panful into a food processor. Process
and then strain. Return the puree to the pan.

3 Meanwhile, mix the cornstarch with 2
tablespoons cold water, working it until you
have a thin, milky liquid, then stir it into
the puree.

4 Bring the pan back to a boil, beating with a
wooden spoon to make sure no lumps form.
Simmer for 3-4 minutes, or until the puree thickens
a little (it will thicken more as it cools).

5 Divide the puree among the serving bowls
and sprinkle the surface with sugar (this stops
a skin from forming). Chill in the refrigerator. To
serve, float a thin layer of cream over the top and
finish with few of the reserved berries.

Blueberry Soup

Serves 4–6

1¼ pounds blueberries
7 ounces sugar
1 heaping tablespoon cornstarch

To serve hot
Crisp bacon, crumbled
Maple syrup

To serve chilled
Whipping cream
Crushed toasted hazelnuts

1 Mash the berries with a potato masher and push the puree through a strainer. Alternatively, put them in a food processor and process until smooth, then push the puree through a strainer. The yield will be around 1½ cups of juice.

2 Meanwhile, make a sugar syrup: put the sugar in a small pan with ⅔ cup water and heat gently, stirring until the sugar is dissolved.

3 Mix the cornstarch with 1 tablespoon water, working it until smooth.

4 Combine the juice and the syrup in a saucepan, stir in the cornstarch and heat gently until it boils. Bubble up, stirring to avoid lumps, for 2–3 minutes, or until the mixture thickens.

5 To serve hot as a first course, ladle into bowls and finish with crisp bacon pieces and a trickle of maple syrup. To serve cold, cover with plastic wrap and set in the refrigerator until well chilled. Ladle into pretty glasses and top with whipping cream and a sprinkle of golden toasted hazelnuts (as pictured to the left).

Quince Soup with
Honey, Wine & Cream

Serves 4–6

2 pounds ripe quinces
2 cups white wine
1 tablespoon honey
2 egg yolks
$\frac{1}{2}$ cup light whipping cream
Salt and ground black pepper

To serve
Seeds of 1 pomegranate
1 tablespoon flaked almonds

Tip
When raw, the quince is pale-fleshed, rock-hard and difficult to peel; when cooked, the flesh softens to a pretty pink and releases a delicate flowery fragrance.

1 Preheat the oven to 350°F. Arrange the quinces on a baking sheet (no need to cut or peel) and bake them until soft; allow 30–40 minutes depending on size. The flesh should be soft. To test if they are done, pierce with a sharp knife.

2 Skin, quarter, and core the quinces. Put the flesh in a blender with the wine and the honey. Process thoroughly until smooth.

3 Transfer to a medium saucepan and heat gently until bubbling. Season lightly with salt and pepper—the flavor should be savory rather than sweet. Reduce the heat and simmer for about 10 minutes, or until the alcohol has evaporated and the steam no longer smells of alcohol.

4 Meanwhile, beat the egg yolks and the cream together until well blended, then stir in a ladleful of the hot soup.

5 Remove the pan from the heat and stir in the cream and egg mixture. Serve without reheating. To serve, sprinkle with pomegranate seeds and flaked almonds.

Danish Buttermilk Soup

Serves 4–6

2 ounces rice flour
2 quarts buttermilk
1 tablespoon raisins (optional)
1 strip of lemon zest
2–3 cardamom pods, roughly crushed
2 eggs, forked to blend
1 tablespoon sugar

To serve
Toasted almonds or croûtons fried in
    butter (see p.224)

1 Mix the rice flour to a paste with 1 tablespoon of the cold buttermilk. Put the remainder of the buttermilk in a saucepan and whisk in the rice mixture. Add the raisins if using, the lemon zest, and cardamom pods.

2 Set the pan over a medium heat and bring gently to a boil. Reduce the heat and stir until the soup thickens and the rice loses its rawness, about 10 minutes. Keep stirring throughout; milk sticks and burns easily. Remove the lemon zest and cardamom pods, if you can find them.

3 Meanwhile, whisk the eggs with the sugar in a separate large bowl.

4 When the soup is ready, pour it into the egg mixture in a thin stream, whisking steadily. Allow to cool, cover with plastic wrap to stop a skin from forming and chill. Serve sprinkled with toasted almonds. In winter, serve hot with crisp croûtons fried in butter. As a pick-me-up, stir in a generous shot of schnapps.

Apricot Soup

with Hazelnuts

Serves 4–6

8 ounces dried apricots, soaked
 overnight
Juice and finely-grated zest of 1 lemon
$\frac{1}{2}$ cup sugar
Pinch of ground ginger
1 tablespoon apricot brandy (optional)

To finish
2 tablespoons toasted hazelnuts
2 tablespoons fresh bread crumbs
1 tablespoon unsalted butter

1 Put the apricots in a saucepan with 1 quart of water, including the remains of the soaking water. Bring to a boil, turn down the heat, and simmer gently until soft.

2 Rub the apricots and their juice through a strainer or puree in an electric blender (blenders always bleach the contents, so they will not be such a deep color). Add the lemon juice and zest, sugar, ginger, and if using, brandy. Reheat (or let chill) and ladle into bowls. Equally good hot or cold.

3 Finish with a sprinkle of toasted hazelnuts and bread crumbs fried crisp in butter.

Rosemary & Lemon

Syllabub

Serves 4–6

½ cup white wine
1 rosemary sprig
2 tablespoons superfine sugar
Juice of 1 lemon
1 cup chilled heavy cream
1 tablespoon brandy

1 Heat the white wine in a small pan, removing it just before it comes to a boil, and add the rosemary. Allow to infuse for 10 minutes. Strain and stir in the sugar and lemon juice.

2 Whisk the cream until it begins to hold its shape—don't overwhip, or it will turn to butter. Whisk in the brandy, and spoon the syllabub into long glasses. Serve immediately, before the wine and the cream have a chance to separate. Serve with ladyfingers or brandy snaps.

Zabaglione

Serves 4–6

6 egg yolks
6 tablespoons superfine sugar
6–8 tablespoons Marsala or sweet
white wine

Tip

If the zabaglione is to be
eaten immediately and you
have no fear of consuming
raw eggs (see p.4), then
there really is no need to
cook it at all.

1 Set a pan of water on to boil—choose one wide enough to take a medium-sized heatproof bowl. In the bowl, beat the egg yolks with the sugar until they are light and fluffy. This will take twice as long as you think.

2 Beat in the Marsala or sweet white wine. Rest the bowl over the now-boiling water. Beat until the mixture is firm and holds the mark of the whisk. Serve in tall glasses to eat with a long spoon.

Chocolate Cream Soup

Serves 4

4 tablespoons powdered chocolate
(unsweetened is best)

1 teaspoon cornstarch

1 short cinnamon stick

1 egg yolk, forked to blend

4 tablespoons condensed milk (or
light cream)

Sugar to taste

1 Stir the chocolate and cornstarch with 2 tablespoons of water in a cup until smooth. Measure 2 cups of water into a pan, stir in the chocolate mixture, add the cinnamon stick, bring to a boil, and whisk over the heat until it thickens a little—4-5 minutes. Remove from the heat and take out the cinnamon.

2 Fork together the egg yolk and condensed milk or cream and whisk the mixture into the hot liquid. Add sugar to taste. Serve with doughnuts—or Spanish churros—for dunking.

Tip

For an extra chocoholic twist, why not add some chocolate shavings before serving. Simply run a vegetable peeler across the edge of a bar of chocolate to create chocolate curls.

Mango Water

Serves 2–4

2 large ripe mangoes
2 tablespoons superfine sugar
$\frac{1}{2}$ teaspoon ground ginger
$\frac{1}{4}$ teaspoon saffron threads

1 Remove the skin and stones from the mangoes —cut straight down either side of the stone and carve the flesh away from the skin from the inside.

2 Drop the mango pulp and the remaining ingredients in a food processor or blender and process to a puree. Store in the refrigerator and dilute to taste with chilled water.

Saffron Milk

Serves 4–6

1¼ quarts milk
About 10 white peppercorns,
  roughly crushed
About 10 saffron threads

To finish
4 tablespoons blanched almonds
4 tablespoons superfine sugar
2 tablespoons poppy seeds
2 tablespoons fennel seeds
½ teaspoon cardamom seeds

1 In a saucepan warm the milk to blood temperature, add the crushed peppercorns and saffron, and leave in a cool place to infuse for 3-4 hours.

2 Meanwhile, in a nut mill or grinder process the almonds to a fine powder with the sugar, poppy seeds, fennel, and cardamom seeds.

3 Strain the milk and stir in the almond powder. Allow to stand for another hour, then strain again, if desired. Serve well chilled.

Wine Soup

with Cinnamon & Cloves

Serves 2–4

1 bottle white wine
2–3 cloves
1 short cinnamon stick
Zest of 1 orange
1–2 tablespoons sugar (depending on
   the sweetness of the wine)
2 eggs

1 Bring the wine to a boil with the spices, orange zest, and sugar.

2 Meanwhile, beat the eggs in a roomy bowl. Take the pan off the heat, remove the spices and zest, and pour the contents from a height into the beaten eggs. Whisk well until it forms a froth. Serve with a crisp cookie or a slice of cake. You can make it with beer if you prefer: perfect with pickled cucumbers and toasted cheese.

Tip

Sweet soups made with
wine, beer, or fruit are served
before the meat in Germany,
in the usual order for soup.
In Finland such sweet soups
are served at the end of
the meal.

Portuguese Sopa
Dorada

Serves 4–6

2½ cups superfine sugar
2–3 slices sponge cake
2 tablespoons orange-flower water
8 egg yolks
2 tablespoons ground almonds

To finish
1 tablespoon ground cinnamon
2 tablespoons sliced, blanched
  almonds
2 tablespoons diced candied fruit
  or grated dark chocolate

1 In a small heavy pan, dissolve the sugar in ½ cup water over a low heat. Boil it rapidly until it reaches the thread stage (220°F—use a sugar thermometer until you get used to the texture). Meanwhile, dice the sponge cake into bite-sized pieces and place in the bottom of a glass serving bowl or divide among 6–8 individual glasses.

2 As soon the syrup is ready, remove a ladleful of the syrup and pour it over the sponge cake.

3 Return the pan to the heat, stir in the orange-flower water, and bring the syrup back to a boil. Bubble it up rapidly until a drop on a saucer forms a skin and wrinkles when you push it with your finger.

4 Meanwhile, in a bowl, whisk the egg yolks together to blend. Whisk in a spoonful of hot syrup. Whisk in the rest of the syrup and pour the mixture back into the pan. Add the ground almonds and stir over a gentle heat until the mixture thickens to the consistency of confectioner's custard. Pour the custard over the sponge cake and finish with a dusting of cinnamon, almonds, and candied fruit or chocolate (very popular in Portugal). Good with whipped cream.

ACCOMPANIMENTS

- Croûtons
- Parsley Dumplings
- Soft Egg Noodles
- Wontons
- Piroshki
- Cobbler Croûte
- Potato Dumplings
- Aïoli
- Almond All-i-oli
- Rouille
- Pesto
- Poppy Seed Rolls
- Salsa Romesco
- Salsa Piri-piri
- Salsa Picante
- Puff Pastry Croûte
- Cheese Straws
- Salt Crackers
- Pita Bread
- Garlic Bread
- Catalan Bread & Tomato
- Oatcakes
- Tortilla Chips
- Melba Toasts
- Sizzling Rice Crisps
- Parmesan Crisps
- Potato Pooris

CHAPTER NINE

ACCOMPANIMENTS

Croûtons

Serves 4

About 2 tablespoons olive oil or butter
1 cup diced stale bread

Optional extras
1 tablespoon diced bacon
1 clove garlic, slivered

1 Heat the oil or butter in a small saucepan, wait until a faint blue haze rises, and sprinkle in the diced bread and either of the optional extras.

2 Toss them in the hot fat until they gild and crisp, then transfer to paper towels to drain. (The smaller the dice, the quicker they will cook).

Parsley Dumplings

Serves 4-6

1 cup all-purpose flour
$\frac{1}{2}$ teaspoon baking powder
2 tablespoons suet (about 2 ounces)
1 heaping tablespoon finely chopped
   fresh parsley
Salt and ground black pepper

1 Work all the ingredients into a soft dough with 1-2 tablespoons of water.

2 Divide the dough into 12 pieces, work each piece into a ball, and drop them gently into boiling water or meat broth. Allow to simmer for 25-30 minutes, or until firm and light.

Soft Egg Noodles

Serves 4–6

1 cup all-purpose flour
½ teaspoon salt
2 eggs

1 Sift the flour with the salt into a bowl. Crack in the eggs, one by one, working each egg thoroughly into the flour using a wooden spoon to avoid lumps, until you have a runny wet dough.

2 You now need a small wooden board with a handle (the wrong side of a butter bat will do) and a blunt knife for cutting the dough into slivers.

3 Bring the broth to which you wish to add the noodles, or a large pan of salted water, to a rolling boil.

4 Spread a couple of spoonfuls of the egg paste on to the end of the dough board. Using the full length of the knife blade, flick slivers of the paste into the boiling liquid, no more than will cover the surface of the water. Alternatively, press the dough through a colander with large holes; do it from a height, or you will find the holes quickly clog up with cooked dough. Wait until the noodles puff up and firm, 1–2 minutes.

5 If you have cooked them in broth, the soup is now ready to serve. If you are cooking the noodles in water and intend to add them to a soup later, scoop them up with a slotted spoon, drop them into a warm bowl, and dress with a little oil or butter to keep them from sticking together.

Wontons

Makes about 24

2 cups all-purpose flour
1 egg
About 6 tablespoons cold water

For the filling
8 ounces finely minced pork
2 tablespoons finely chopped scallions
1 teaspoon finely chopped fresh
    root ginger
2 tablespoons light soy sauce
$\frac{1}{2}$ teaspoon sesame oil
$\frac{1}{2}$ teaspoon sugar

1 First make the dough. Sift the flour into a roomy bowl, make a well in the middle with your fist and crack in the egg. Add the water. Work the wet ingredients into the flour thoroughly with your hand —or use a food processor with the dough-hook attached—until you have a smooth, elastic but still quite firm dough. This will take about 10 minutes of kneading. Form into a ball. Cover with plastic wrap and set aside for 30 minutes to rest.

2 Meanwhile prepare the filling. Mix all the filling ingredients together, kneading thoroughly with your hands, until well combined. Set aside in a cool place until the dough has rested.

3 On a lightly floured board, using long strokes of a rolling pin, roll out the dough ball into a thin sheet—you should be able to see the grain of the wood through the dough. Divide the sheet into 24 squares, each about the width of your hand.

4 Holding one of the squares in the palm of your hand, drop a teaspoonful of filling into the middle. Wet the uncovered part of the dough and bring the edges together to enclose the filling, leaving the ends loose, like a pocket handkerchief. Transfer to a lightly floured baking tray and continue until the dough and the filling are all used up.

5 To cook, bring a panful of broth to a rolling boil and slip in the wontons one at a time so that the temperature doesn't drop. Simmer for 6–10 minutes to ensure the filling is cooked right through.

Piroshki

Serves 8–10

2½ cups all-purpose flour
1 teaspoon salt
2 eggs
1 teaspoon oil
About 2 tablespoons cold water

For the filling
1 small onion, finely chopped
1 tablespoon butter or lard
1½ cups mushrooms, diced
1 teaspoon chopped fresh parsley
½ teaspoon freshly grated nutmeg
1 egg
2 tablespoons fresh curd cheese
   (feta, ricotta)
Salt and ground black pepper

1 First make the wrapper dough. Sift the flour and salt into a bowl and make a well in the middle with your fist. Crack in the eggs and add the oil. Mix the wet ingredients into the dry—easily done with an electric mixer—and add enough water to make a softish dough. Knead vigorously— massage it with your knuckles and the flat of your hand—until smooth and no longer sticky. Flour the dough lightly, and drop it into a plastic bag. Set aside to rest for 30 minutes.

2 Meanwhile, make the filling. Fry the onion gently in the butter or lard, until it softens and takes a little color. Stir in the mushrooms and cook them until their moisture has all evaporated. Stir in the parsley and nutmeg and add salt and pepper. Let cool. When you are ready to stuff the piroshki, mix in the egg and the curd cheese.

3 Roll out the dough thinly on a well-floured board, and cut out 2-inch diameter rounds. Put a teaspoon of filling in the middle of each round, wet the edges and fold in half, pressing the edges together to enclose the filling. Continue until all is used up.

4 Bring a large pan of salted water (or the broth in which you mean to float the dumplings) to a boil. Drop the piroshki, a few at a time. Wait till they bob to the surface, and cook for a further 2 minutes.

Cobbler Croûte

Serves 4-6

5 cups all-purpose flour
$\frac{1}{2}$ teaspoon baking soda
$\frac{1}{2}$ teaspoon salt
$\frac{1}{2}$ stick (4 tablespoons) butter
About 1 cup milk or buttermilk

1 Sift the flour, baking soda, and salt into a bowl and rub in the butter with your fingertips. Fork in the liquid. The mixture should be wet—the wetter the mix, the lighter the dough. Push it together to form a soft ball. Pat it out to the thickness of your hand and cut out rounds using a wine glass. Repeat with the scraps.

2 Fill an ovenproof tureen or a casserole right to the top with soup—you need something thick and robust—and leave aside to cool and set (a cobbler topping prefers a firm surface). Or fill small bowls, if you would like to serve individual portions. Meanwhile, preheat the oven to 400°F.

3 Lay the rounds of dough over the set surface, overlapping them so that the entire surface is covered and sticking down the overlap with a damp finger.

4 Bake for 20 minutes to set the pastry, then cover with foil, lower the heat, and continue to cook until you are sure the soup inside is really hot.

Potato Dumplings

Makes about 16

8 ounces floury potatoes, unpeeled
1 tablespoon butter
1 egg
1 cup all-purpose flour

1 Boil the potatoes in their jackets until soft. Skin them while still hot and mash them with butter until smooth. Let cool for 10 minutes.

2 Work in the egg. Sift the flour on to a kneading board (or directly on to a clean tabletop) and tip out the dough. Knead the potato with the flour until you have a soft pliable dough—you may not need all the flour. Cover with plastic wrap and set aside for 30 minutes.

3 Divide the dough into 16 pieces. Work each piece into a ball.

4 Bring a panful of broth to a boil—or you can cook them in salted water if you prefer. Gently lower the dumplings into the boiling liquid, only as many as will comfortably cover the surface. Bring back to simmering point and simmer steadily for 10–12 minutes, or until the dumplings are firm. To save and add to a soup later, remove the dumplings to a colander and rinse gently with cold water.

Aïoli

Serves 4

2–4 plump firm cloves garlic
1 teaspoon sea salt
2 large egg yolks
About 2¹⁄₂ cups mild olive oil
Juice of 1 lemon

1 Make sure all the ingredients are at room-temperature before you begin (this is always important when making an emulsion).

2 Reduce the garlic to a fine paste by pounding it with the salt using a pestle in a mortar. Work in the egg yolks. Add the oil very slowly at first, blending with the pestle or using a wooden spoon. As it thickens you can increase the flow of oil, continuing to work it until the aïoli thickens to the consistency of soft butter. Add the lemon juice cautiously at the end—no need to overwhelm the garlic.

Almond All-i-oli

Serves 4–6

6 cloves garlic, skinned
¹⁄₂ teaspoon sea salt
2 tablespoons blanched almonds, pounded to a paste
1 egg yolk
About 1 cup olive oil
1–2 tablespoons wine vinegar

1 Thoroughly crush the garlic with the salt in a mortar or a bowl. Mix in the almond paste and the egg yolk. Using a wooden spoon or an electric hand mixer (starting slowly and increasing the speed as the sauce thickens), incorporate the olive oil as for a mayonnaise. Add it drop by drop at first, speeding up to a thin stream as the sauce begins to thicken. Add a few drops of vinegar as you work: it helps the emulsion. Taste and add more vinegar if the all-iol-i is not quite sharp enough.

Rouille

Serves 6–8

4 cloves garlic

½ teaspoon salt

2 red bell peppers, whole (or ready-prepared, canned)

1 thick slice dry bread (about 2 ounces)

2 red chiles, seeded and chopped

1 Crush the garlic with the salt. Toast the peppers in a very hot oven (450°F) for about 15 minutes, or burn them over a direct flame until the skin is charred. Pop them into a plastic bag to soften for 20 minutes, then scrape the flesh from the skin with a knife.

2 Soak the bread in a little water and squeeze it dry. Pound all the ingredients together into a smooth paste in a food processor, or with a pestle and mortar.

Tip

This accompaniment works just as well with any of the Mediterranean's vast repertoire of broth-based soups, including those which include vegetables and pulses. Sparked up with a little chile, it adds fieriness as well as color and flavor.

Pesto

Serves 4-6

2 tablespoons (about 1 ounce) pine
  nuts
2 cloves garlic, roughly chopped
1 teaspoon coarse sea salt
4 handfuls of fresh basil (about 2
  ounces, leaves and top sprigs only)
2 ounces freshly grated Parmesan
  cheese
2 ounces freshly grated Pecorino
  cheese
$\frac{1}{3}$ cup extra virgin olive oil

1 Toast the pine nuts lightly in a dry skillet,
2-3 minutes only, to restore perfect freshness.

2 Mortar method: pound the garlic with the salt
until you have a soft, smooth mush. Pound in
the pine nuts. Work in the basil leaves with a
circular movement of the pestle until all is reduced
to a silky paste (at this point the mixture can be
frozen). Work in the cheeses, then beat in the olive
oil using a wooden spoon until you have a thick,
dense sauce.

3 Processor method: drop all the ingredients into
the food processor or blender and process to a
luscious green slick. Easy.

Tip

If storing pesto, omit the
cheese (work it in when you are
ready to serve). Ladle the pesto into a
jar, and float a layer of oil over the top.
Cover and keep it in the refrigerator for
no longer than a week, when it'll
begin to lose its fragrance.
Alternatively, it can be frozen.

Poppy Seed Rolls

Makes 12

6 cups white bread flour
1 teaspoon salt
1 ounce fresh yeast ($\frac{1}{2}$ ounce dried)
1 teaspoon sugar
1 egg
1 cup warm milk
2 tablespoons melted butter

To finish
2–3 tablespoons milk
2–3 heaping tablespoons poppy seeds

1 Sift the flour and salt into a warm bowl.

2 Cream the yeast with the sugar and fork it up with the egg, milk, and melted butter. Pour the yeast mixture into a well in the flour and work it all together. Knead thoroughly until you have a soft, smooth dough—you may need to add more flour. Drop the dough ball back in its bowl, cover with plastic wrap, and set in a warm place to rise for 1 hour, or until doubled in size.

3 Knock back the dough—punch and knead it to distribute the air bubbles—and cut it into three equal pieces. Cut each piece in half and then in half again, yielding 12 pieces. Work each piece into a ball and transfer to a greased baking sheet. Brush the tops with a little milk and sprinkle with the poppy seeds.

4 Cover with oiled plastic wrap—this time make sure the plastic wrap doesn't touch the dough —and set to rise again for another 30 minutes.

5 Bake for 20-25 minutes, or until well-risen and golden. Cool on a wire rack.

Salsa Romesco

Serves 4–6

2 dried red peppers (Ñora), seeded and
  soaked to swell
2 large ripe tomatoes
2 cloves garlic, crushed
1 teaspoon salt
2 tablespoons fresh white bread
  crumbs fried until crisp in a little
  olive oil
2 tablespoons toasted almonds
1 dried red chile, seeded and crumbled
About 1 cup olive oil
2 tablespoons red wine vinegar

1 Roast the dried peppers and the tomatoes under a hot broiler until they blister and take color. Pop them into a plastic bag and let cool. Scrape the pulp from the skin of the peppers, skin the tomatoes, scooping out and discarding the seeds, and drop them into a food processor or blender. Add the garlic, salt, bread crumbs, almonds, and dried red chile and pulverize to a paste (or use a pestle and mortar).

2 Add the oil and the red wine vinegar, and continue to process or pound until the sauce is thick and shiny.

Salsa Piri-piri

Makes about 1 cup

8 ounces fresh red chiles (malagueta
  for preference)
8 ounces mild red bell peppers
4 tablespoons sea salt
$\frac{1}{2}$ cup white wine vinegar

1 Hull the chiles and cut the peppers into strips. Pack them into a sterilized jar with the salt, then seal and leave for a month. Using a food processor or blender process the chiles and peppers with the vinegar and then bottle up the salsa in a sterilized jar. Keep in a dark, cool cupboard and use after 1 week.

Salsa Picante

Makes about 1¼ quarts

8 pounds tomatoes
1 cup vinegar
4 tablespoons brown sugar
1 tablespoon crushed allspice berries
1–3 tablespoons powdered or flaked chile
Salt and ground black pepper

Tip
Mexico's favorite hot sauce. Great in a chilled soup—gazpacho or avocado (see pp.36 and 44)—even better in a bean broth.

1. Roughly chop the tomatoes. Put all the ingredients except the chile into a large saucepan. Add 1 teaspoon salt and allow them to infuse for 30 minutes.

2. Bring the pan to a boil, turn down to a gentle simmer, and allow to cook over a low heat for at least 1 hour (it shouldn't need much attention as the tomatoes produce plenty of liquid at this stage, so there's little danger of sticking).

3. Push the tomato mixture through a fine-meshed strainer, leaving skin, pips, and spice debris behind. Return the puree to the pan.

4. Bring back to a boil and simmer vigorously, stirring regularly, until the sauce is as thick as you like it—this may take as long as 40 minutes.

5. Stir in the chile, adding as much or as little as you like. Adjust the seasoning. Bottle it up in empty tequila bottles and cork tightly.

Puff Pastry Croûte

Serves 4–6

2 cups all-purpose flour
$^1/_2$ teaspoon salt
2 sticks (16 tablespoons) unsalted
   butter
About 2 tablespoons water

1 Make the pastry in a very cool place. Ensure that the butter is firm without being hard. Take a large bowl and sift in the flour with the salt. Cut in $^3/_4$ stick (6 tablespoons) of the butter with a sharp knife until you have a mixture like fine bread crumbs. Mix in enough water to make a paste that does not stick to your fingers. Knead lightly.

2 Set the dough aside for 20 minutes, with the remaining butter beside it so that pastry and butter both reach the same temperature.

3 Roll out the pastry to a thickness of about $^1/_5$-inch. Dot it with small pieces of butter the size of a hazelnut, using about one-third of the total quantity. Then fold the pastry into three, like a napkin, and again into three, with the folds in the opposite direction. Set the pastry aside for 20 minutes.

4 Go through the buttering and folding process twice more, adding the same amount of butter each time. Set the pastry aside for 20 minutes after each process. Then leave it for another 20 minutes before you roll it out. Meanwhile, preheat the oven to 375°F.

5 Cut the pastry into rounds a little larger than the top of your soup bowls, which should be made of robust ovenproof pottery.

6 Fill the bowls with cold soup. Wet the rims and drape a pastry lid over the top, pressing the edge with your thumb to make sure of a good fit. Cut a small cross in the top to allow steam to escape.

7 Bake for 25–30 minutes, or until the pastry is well risen and golden.

Cheese Straws

Makes about 18

2 cups all-purpose flour
½ teaspoon salt
2¼ sticks unsalted butter, frozen
8 ounces hard cheese (Cheddar or
   similar), grated
1 egg yolk, forked to blend

1 Sift the flour and salt into a chilled bowl. Grate the butter into the flour, working quickly so that the butter remains firm. Fork in the grated cheese. Make a dip in the middle and drop in the egg yolk. Press the dough together with your fingertips until it forms a soft mass—you may need a little iced water (it depends on the butter and the temperature of the kitchen). Don't overwork the dough or the butter will oil, and you will need extra flour and the dough will toughen.

2 Drop the dough into a plastic bag and let it rest and firm in the refrigerator for at least 30 minutes—overnight is best. Preheat the oven to 375°F and grease a baking sheet.

3 Press the dough ball gently with a rolling pin to flatten, and sandwich it between two sheets of plastic wrap. Using short strokes of the rolling pin, gently press it out to a rectangle about the thickness of your little finger. Cut the rectangle into about 18 long, narrow fingers. Transfer the fingers to the baking sheet.

4 Bake for about 20 minutes, or until golden and perfectly dry. Transfer gently to a wire rack to cool and become crisp.

Salt Crackers

Makes about 24

4½ cups white bread flour
⅓ stick (3 tablespoons) butter
1 cup hot water
3 tablespoons milk
1 teaspoon salt crystals

1 Preheat the oven to 375°F and grease a baking sheet. Sift the flour into a large bowl. Melt the butter in the water and stir in the milk. Pour the hot liquid into a well in the flour and mix together until you have quite a stiff dough. Tip out on to a board or table top lightly dusted with flour and knead well until smooth and elastic.

2 Roll the dough out as thin as cardboard. Use a large water glass or cookie cutter to cut the dough into rounds. Prick them with a fork, sprinkle with the salt crystals, and press them into the dough with the flat of your hand. Lay the rounds on the baking sheet.

3 Bake for 7-8 minutes, or until pale gold and crisp. Serve hot. Alternatively, store in an airtight tin and reheat gently to serve.

Pita Bread

Makes 12

5 cups white bread flour
½ teaspoon salt
2 ounces fresh yeast
About 1 cup warm water
1 teaspoon sugar
2 tablespoons plain yogurt
A little oil for greasing
1 tablespoon nigella or sesame seeds
   for dusting (optional)

1 Sift the flour with the salt into a warm bowl. Dissolve the yeast in a splash of the warm water and add a teaspoon of sugar to start it working. As soon as it bubbles up, make a well in the center of the flour and pour in the yeast water. Add the yogurt and draw the dry ingredients into the wet, kneading by hand or with the dough hook on a food processor.

2 Work in enough warm water to make a soft, sticky dough. Knead for about 20 minutes, until it's quite smooth and elastic. Form into a ball and slick it with oil (pour a little into your hand, and swipe it over the dough). Drop the dough back into the bowl, cover with plastic wrap, and allow to rise for 1-2 hours in a warm place, until doubled in size.

3 Knock back the dough using your knuckles and knead it for another 5 minutes. Break off a lump of dough the size of a small egg, work it into a ball, drop it on to a floured board, and flatten it with your palm—the shape should be oval and the length a little longer than your hand. Transfer to another floured board. Continue until all the dough is used up. Cover with plastic wrap and allow to rise for another 20 minutes.

4 Meanwhile, preheat the oven to 425°F. Lightly oil two large baking sheets, dust them with flour, and put them in the oven to heat. As soon as the baking sheets are smoking hot, transfer the pita breads to the baking sheets, sprinkle them with water using your fingers, and dust with the seeds if using.

5 Bake for 6-12 minutes, or until puffed and blistered—they are done when they smell earthy. Transfer to a clean cloth and wrap them up to keep them soft.

Garlic Bread

Serves 4–6

1 day-old baguette
2 cloves garlic, mashed
About ¾ stick (6 tablespoons) unsalted
   butter, softened

1 Preheat the oven to 350°F. Cut six diagonal slits in the baguette without cutting through to the base. Mash the garlic with the butter until well blended.

2 Fill the slashes with the garlicky butter—the fresher the garlic, the gentler the flavor. Sprinkle the crust with a little water.

3 Wrap the baguette in aluminum foil and bake for about 20 minutes, until the butter has melted into the crumb. Open the package and bake for another 5 minutes to crispen the crust.

Catalan Bread & Tomato

Serves 4

2 large, firm, ripe tomatoes
4 thick slices chewy sourdough bread
1–2 fat, firm cloves garlic, halved
4 tablespoons extra virgin olive oil
Sea salt

1 Preheat the oven to 450°F, lay the tomatoes on a baking sheet and roast for 15–20 minutes, until perfectly soft. Slip them out of their skins and mash the pulp a little. If the tomatoes are field-grown and ripened on the vine, you can use them raw.

2 Meanwhile, broil the bread over a high heat— the crumb should blacken a little. Rub with a cut clove of garlic, trickle generously with oil, and spread thickly with tomato pulp, pushing it well into the bread. Or crush the garlic to a pulp and sprinkle it over the top. Finish with a few grains of salt. You can, if you like, present all the elements separately for people to prepare their own.

Oatcakes

Makes about 24

8 ounces fine-ground oatmeal
8 ounces coarse-ground oatmeal
½ teaspoon salt
2–3 tablespoons melted bacon dripping
   or lard
About 1 cup boiling water

Tip

Fine-ground oatmeal gives a smooth crisp oatcake suitable for tea, and a proportion of coarse-ground oatmeal, as here, gives a crunchy texture suitable for eating with soup. Make sure you have oatmeal—porridge-oats won't do. Butter or oil can replace the traditional lard or dripping as shortening.

1 Preheat the oven to 300°F, and grease a baking sheet.

2 Toss the two oatmeals in a bowl with the salt. Mash in the drippings or lard and work in enough water to make a firm dough.

3 Pat the dough out between two sheets of plastic wrap and roll out to ⅛-inch thick. Cut into squares about the size of your palm.

4 Transfer the squares to a baking sheet and bake for 25–35 minutes, until dry—don't let them brown. Transfer to a cooling rack. They will crisp up as they cool. Store in an airtight tin. If they soften, warm them up again in a low oven.

Tortilla Chips

Serves 4–6

4 small maize-flour tortillas (or 2 large
   wheat-flour tortillas)
Oil, for shallow frying

1 Using a sharp knife or kitchen scissors, cut the tortillas into bite-sized pieces. For totopos, cut the tortilla into squares; for nachos, cut it into triangles.

2 Heat a finger's depth of oil in a small skillet and drop in the tortilla pieces. Fry, turning them with a slotted spoon, until crisp and lightly browned. Transfer to paper towel and pat to remove the excess oil.

Tip

You can add these to a soup in much the same way as croûtons, or serve them as a nibble on the side. They are, of course, available from a packet. But if you fry your own, there's no need to worry about over-saltiness and you can choose the oil you like best.

Melba Toasts

Makes 8 slices

4 thick slices day-old white bread

1 Toast the bread lightly on both sides. Remove the crusts and split the slices in two by slipping a sharp knife gently through the soft crumb, leaving you with eight thin slices toasted on one side only.

2 Toast the crumb side either under a slow broiler or in the oven preheated to 350°F for 10–15 minutes, or until perfectly dry, brittle, and brown. You can, if you prefer, simply dry out thin slices of bread in the oven until brittle and lightly browned—not strictly Melba since it will lack the characteristic roughness, but still good as an accompaniment to soup.

Tip

Melba toast keeps well in an airtight container and can be gently reheated to re-awaken its freshness and flavor.

Sizzling Rice Crisps

Makes 12

2 cups ready-cooked white rice
   (sticky enough to form lumps)
Oil, for shallow frying

1 Spread the rice on a baking sheet—don't break up the lumps—and allow to dry out at room temperature overnight. Alternatively, bake in a low oven for 10-15 minutes, or spread in a glass baking dish and microwave on Low for 10 minutes.

2 Heat a finger's depth of oil in a small skillet until a faint blue haze rises. Drop in the rice lumps in small batches and pat them gently with a spatula to form a biscuit shape. Wait until they are crisp and lightly browned, about 3-4 minutes, turning them as they fry. Remove and drain on paper towels.

Parmesan Crisps

Makes 8–10

8 ounces Parmesan or Pecorino cheese, thickly grated or 8 ounces Cheddar cheese, grated 1 day ahead and left to dry out overnight.

1 Heat a griddle or small skillet over a high heat—an omelet pan is perfect.

2 When the pan is good and hot, sprinkle the base with a thin layer of grated cheese. Squish it down with a fork as it melts and crisps. When you have a nice brown, lacy pancake, flick it over and cook the other side for a few seconds. You can, if you prefer, fry tablespoons of the grated cheese in shallow oil—keep stirring with a fork and the scraps of cheese will stick together as they melt and harden.

Potato Pooris

Makes 8

1 medium potato, freshly boiled in
   its jacket
1½ cups all-purpose flour
½ teaspoon salt
½ teaspoon ground cumin
½ teaspoon garam masala or your
   favorite curry powder
4 teaspoons sesame oil
Oil for frying

1 Skin the potato as soon as it's cool enough to handle and mash in a bowl. Mix in the flour, salt, and spices. Work in the sesame oil with a little water and knead for 10 minutes to give a firm ball of dough—or drop it in a food processor or blender and work with the dough-hook until smooth. Work it into a ball, wrap in plastic wrap and set aside for 15 minutes to rest.

2 Knead the dough again and divide it into 8 pieces. Knead each piece into a ball. Cover.

3 Flour a board and a rolling pin, pat out each ball into a round, and then roll it out to the size of a side plate—6 inches. Or sandwich each dough-ball between 2 sheets of plastic wrap (no flour necessary) and press rather than roll until you achieve the same result. Continue until all are rolled.

4 Heat a finger's depth of oil in a wide skillet. When the oil is lightly hazed with blue, slip the first poori into the hot oil—bubbles should form immediately round the edge. Keep tapping it with the back of a slotted spoon so that it's just pushed under the oil. Within a few seconds it will balloon up. Flip it over and fry the other side for a few seconds, until very lightly browned. Remove with a slotted spoon and transfer to paper towels. Continue until all the pooris are done.

Index